GREAT AMERICAN
P·I·E·S

PUBLICATIONS INTERNATIONAL, LTD.

INTRODUCTION

Pies—glorious pies! From across the land, America's bounty provides the inspiration for this collection of taste-tempting pie recipes. There are savory, satisfying main dishes like southern Deep-Dish Chicken Pot Pie or Maine's Downeast Clam Pie, plus dozens of scrumptious dessert pies to round out any meal perfectly. Try cool Key Lime Pie from Florida or Traditional Pumpkin Pie from the midwestern heartland.

In addition to these popular regional pies, you'll find wonderful creations sure to please every palate. Chocolate lovers can indulge in rich, fudgy chocolate pies of all kinds. Traditional pie eaters will enjoy favorites like ReaLemon Meringue and Coconut Custard pies. And on a hot summer's day, everyone will revel in refreshing Pink Lemonade, Fresh Strawberry and Frozen Orange Cloud pies.

So, pick a Great American Pie to celebrate every season and every occasion . . . and enjoy!

IF IT'S BORDEN-IT'S
GOT TO BE GOOD®

© 1990 Borden, Inc.

Some Borden products are in limited distribution.

All recipes developed and tested by the home economists of the Borden Kitchens.

Director, Borden Kitchens: Annie Watts Cloncs
Photography Coordination: Partners in Promotion, Inc.

ISBN: 0-88176-908-8

Library of Congress Catalog Card Number: 90-60061

This edition published by:
Publications International, Ltd.
7373 N. Cicero Avenue
Lincolnwood, IL 60646

Pictured on the front cover: ReaLemon Meringue Pie *(page 74)*.

Pictured on the back cover *(clockwise from top left)*: Cheeseburger Pie *(page 7)*, Cherry Cheese Pie *(page 66)*, Frozen Margarita Pie with Frozen Strawberry Margarita Pie *(page 55)* and Harvest Fruit Custard Tart *(page 24)*.

Manufactured in Yugoslavia.

h g f e d c b a

GREAT AMERICAN P·I·E·S

Microwave Cooking

Microwave ovens vary in wattage and power output; cooking times given with microwave directions in this book may need to be adjusted.

A Note About Eggs

Some recipes in this book specify, "Use only Grade A clean, uncracked eggs." This is a precaution given when uncooked or partially cooked eggs are called for, such as in meringues or pie fillings.

SAVORY ⋆ BA

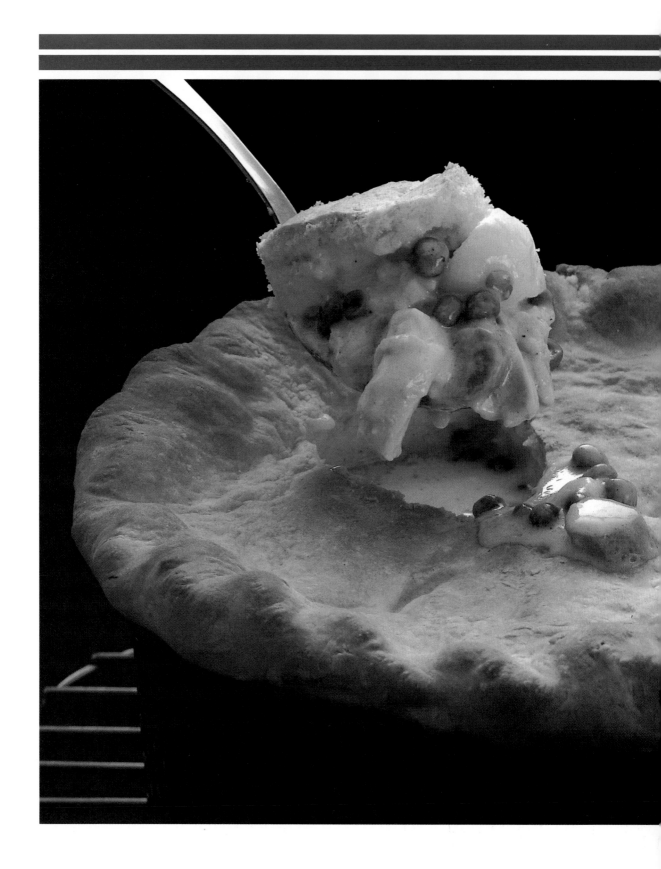

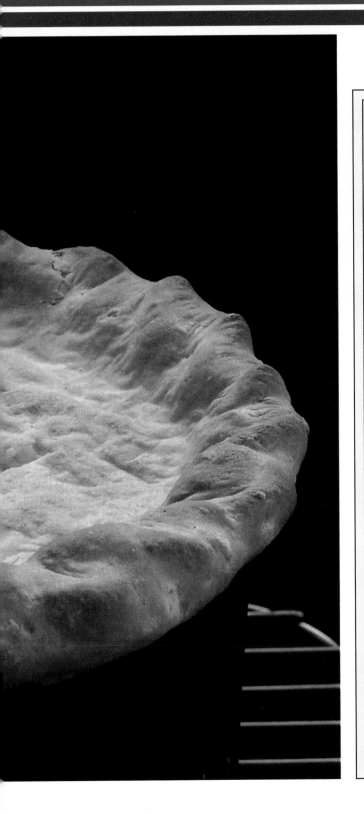

For a satisfying supper, light luncheon entree or tantalizing party tidbit, serve a savory pie. Enjoy the hearty goodness of classics like Deep-Dish Chicken Pot Pie, or choose a flavorful quiche for special main-dish fare.

Pictured here is Deep-Dish Chicken Pot Pie; see page 6 for recipe.

★★★★
DEEP-DISH CHICKEN POT PIE

Makes 6 servings

3 cups cubed cooked chicken
1 cup sliced cooked carrots
   (2 medium)
1 cup cubed cooked potatoes
   (1 medium)
1 cup frozen green peas, thawed
6 tablespoons margarine or butter
⅓ cup unsifted flour
2 tablespoons Wyler's® or Steero®
   Chicken-Flavor Instant
   Bouillon *or* 6 Chicken-Flavor
   Bouillon Cubes
⅛ to ¼ teaspoon pepper
4 cups Borden® or Meadow
   Gold® Milk
2¼ cups biscuit baking mix

Preheat oven to 375°. In large saucepan, melt margarine; stir in flour, bouillon and pepper. Over medium heat, gradually add milk; cook and stir until thickened. Add remaining ingredients except biscuit mix. Pour into 2½-quart baking dish. Prepare biscuit mix according to package directions for rolled biscuits. Roll out to cover top of dish; cut slits near center. Place dough over filling; turn under edge, seal and flute. Bake 40 minutes or until golden. Refrigerate leftovers.

★★★★
FRENCH ONION MUSHROOM QUICHE

Makes one 9-inch quiche

1 (9-inch) unbaked pastry shell
1 large sweet onion, thinly sliced
   (about 1 pound)
2 cups sliced fresh mushrooms
   (about 8 ounces)
¼ cup margarine or butter
2 tablespoons flour
1 cup (4 ounces) shredded Swiss
   cheese
4 eggs
1 cup Borden® or Meadow Gold®
   Half-and-Half or Milk
1 tablespoon Wyler's® or Steero®
   Beef-Flavor Instant Bouillon
Canned French fried onions

Preheat oven to 425°. Bake pastry shell 8 minutes; remove from oven. Reduce oven temperature to 350°. Meanwhile, in large skillet, on medium-high heat, cook onion and mushrooms in margarine until liquid evaporates. Remove from heat; stir in flour until smooth. Sprinkle about ½ cup cheese into prepared pastry shell; add onion-mushroom mixture. In medium bowl, beat eggs, half-and-half and bouillon; stir in remaining cheese. Pour over onion-mushroom mixture. Bake 30 minutes or until set. Top with French fried onions last 5 minutes of baking. Let stand 10 minutes before serving. Refrigerate leftovers.

TO MAKE AHEAD: Prepare as above, omitting French fried onions; cool. Cover and refrigerate overnight. Heat in preheated 325° oven 45 minutes or until hot. Top with French fried onions last 5 minutes of baking.

★★★★

CHEESEBURGER PIE

Makes one 9-inch pie

1 (9-inch) unbaked pastry shell
8 slices Borden® Process
    American Cheese Food
1 pound lean ground beef
½ cup tomato sauce
⅓ cup chopped green bell pepper
⅓ cup chopped onion
1 teaspoon Wyler's® or Steero®
    Beef-Flavor Instant Bouillon
    or 1 Beef-Flavor Bouillon
    Cube
3 eggs, beaten
2 tablespoons flour
    Chopped tomato and shredded
    lettuce, optional

Preheat oven to 425°. Bake pastry shell 8 minutes. Remove from oven. Reduce oven temperature to 350°. Meanwhile, cut *6 slices* cheese food into pieces. In large skillet, brown meat; pour off fat. Add tomato sauce, green pepper, onion and bouillon; cook and stir until bouillon dissolves. Remove from heat; stir in eggs, flour and cheese food pieces. Turn into prepared pastry shell. Bake 20 to 25 minutes or until hot. Arrange remaining *2 slices* cheese food on top. Return to oven 3 minutes or until cheese food begins to melt. Garnish with tomato and lettuce if desired. Refrigerate leftovers.

SWISS SALMON QUICHE

Makes one 9-inch quiche

1 (9-inch) unbaked pastry shell
¾ cup finely chopped onion
2 tablespoons margarine or butter
1½ cups (6 ounces) shredded Swiss
    cheese
1 (7-ounce) can salmon *or* tuna,
    drained and flaked
1 tablespoon ReaLemon® Lemon
    Juice from Concentrate
3 eggs
1 (8-ounce) container Borden® or
    Meadow Gold® Sour Cream
1 tablespoon flour
2 teaspoons Wyler's® or Steero®
    Chicken-Flavor Instant
    Bouillon
¼ cup chopped green bell pepper

Preheat oven to 425°. Bake pastry shell 8 minutes; remove from oven. Reduce oven temperature to 350°. Meanwhile, in small saucepan, cook onion in margarine until tender. Arrange cheese in bottom of prepared pastry shell. Toss salmon with ReaLemon® brand; spoon over cheese. In medium bowl, beat eggs, sour cream, onion mixture, flour and bouillon; pour over salmon. Top with green pepper. Bake 30 minutes or until golden brown. Let stand 10 minutes before serving. Refrigerate leftovers.

TO MAKE AHEAD: Prepare as above; cool. Cover and refrigerate overnight. Heat in preheated 325° oven 45 minutes or until hot.

DEEP-DISH COTTAGE PIZZA

Makes one 15×10-inch pizza

1 (16-ounce) package hot roll mix
½ pound bulk hot Italian sausage
1 clove garlic, finely chopped
1 (16-ounce) container Borden®
    or Meadow Gold® Cottage
    Cheese
1 (12-ounce) can tomato paste
½ cup chopped onion
1 teaspoon oregano leaves
1 teaspoon salt
½ cup chopped green bell pepper
½ cup grated Parmesan cheese

Prepare roll mix and let rise as package directs. Press on bottom and up sides of greased 15×10-inch jellyroll pan. In skillet, cook sausage and garlic; pour off fat. In medium bowl, combine cottage cheese, tomato paste, onion, oregano and salt; spread in prepared pan. Top with sausage, green pepper and grated cheese. Let rise 30 minutes. Bake in preheated 375° oven 35 minutes. Refrigerate leftovers.

Deep-Dish Cottage Pizza

★ ★ ★ ★

POTATO BURGER PIE

Makes one 9-inch pie

1 pound lean ground beef
½ cup plain dry bread crumbs
1 egg, beaten
¼ cup ketchup
1 teaspoon Wyler's® or Steero®
 Beef-Flavor Instant Bouillon
⅛ teaspoon pepper
4 cups frozen hash brown
 potatoes
½ cup chopped onion
1 (2½-ounce) jar sliced
 mushrooms, drained
1 (8-ounce) package Fisher®
 Ched-O-Mate® or Pizza-
 Mate® Shredded Cheese
 Substitute

Preheat oven to 350°. In large bowl, combine meat, crumbs, egg, ketchup, bouillon and pepper; press on bottom and side to rim of 9-inch pie plate. Combine potatoes, onion, mushrooms and *½ cup* cheese substitute; spoon over meat. Cover; bake 45 minutes. Pour off fat. Top with remaining *1½ cups* cheese substitute; bake 5 minutes longer or until melted. Garnish as desired. Refrigerate leftovers.

★ ★ ★ ★

MINI QUICHES

Makes 24 quiches

½ cup margarine or butter,
    softened
1 (3-ounce) package cream cheese,
    softened
1⅔ cups unsifted flour
1½ cups Borden® or Meadow Gold®
    Sour Cream
¾ cup (3 ounces) shredded Swiss
    cheese
2 eggs, beaten
3 tablespoons finely chopped
    onion
2 teaspoons Wyler's® or Steero®
    Chicken-Flavor Instant
    Bouillon
¼ teaspoon ground nutmeg
2 slices bacon, cooked and
    crumbled

Preheat oven to 400°. In large mixer bowl, beat margarine and cream cheese until fluffy; stir in flour. Divide dough into 24 balls. Place each ball of dough in a 2-inch tart pan or muffin cup; press evenly on bottom and up side. In medium bowl, combine remaining ingredients except bacon; mix well. Spoon about 1 tablespoon egg mixture into each tart pan. Sprinkle with bacon. Bake 20 minutes or until golden. Serve warm. Refrigerate leftovers.

TIP: Quiches can be baked ahead, tightly wrapped and stored in freezer. To reheat, bake frozen quiches in preheated 350° oven 12 to 15 minutes.

★ ★ ★ ★

GRECIAN
CHICKEN PIE

Makes 8 to 10 servings

4 cups cubed cooked chicken
2 cups sliced fresh mushrooms
    (about 8 ounces)
½ cup chopped onion
¾ to 1 cup margarine or butter
2 tablespoons flour
1 (14½-ounce) can stewed
    tomatoes, undrained
½ cup water
1 tablespoon Wyler's® or Steero®
    Chicken-Flavor Instant
    Bouillon *or* 3 Chicken-Flavor
    Bouillon Cubes
¼ teaspoon thyme leaves
¼ cup sliced pitted ripe olives
1 (16-ounce) package frozen
    phylo (streudel) pastry leaves,
    thawed
    Grated Parmesan cheese

Preheat oven to 350°. In large skillet, cook mushrooms and onion in *2 tablespoons* margarine until tender. Add flour, stirring until smooth. Add tomatoes, water, bouillon and thyme; cook and stir until bouillon dissolves. Remove from heat; stir in chicken and olives. Melt remaining margarine. Place 2 sheets pastry in bottom of greased 15×10-inch jellyroll pan, pressing into corners. Brush with margarine; repeat using 2 sheets pastry brushed with margarine for each layer, until half of pastry has been used. Spread chicken filling over pastry; repeat layering with pastry sheets and margarine until all the pastry has been used. Trim edges of pastry even with edge of pan. Sprinkle lightly with cheese. Bake 25 minutes or until pastry is golden. Refrigerate leftovers.

★ ★ ★ ★
SALMON CHEESE PUFF PIES

Makes 6 servings

1 (15½-ounce) can salmon, drained and flaked
1 cup Borden® or Meadow Gold® Cottage Cheese
¼ cup chopped green bell pepper
¼ cup chopped onion
3 tablespoons ReaLemon® Lemon Juice from Concentrate
1 (2-ounce) jar pimientos, drained and chopped
¼ teaspoon dill weed
1 (10-ounce) package frozen puff pastry patty shells, thawed in refrigerator overnight

Preheat oven to 450°. In large bowl, combine all ingredients except patty shells. On floured surface, roll each shell to an 8-inch circle. Place equal amounts of salmon mixture in center of each circle. Fold over; seal edges with water and press with fork. Place on ungreased baking sheet; cut slit near center of each turnover. Reduce oven temperature to 400°; bake 25 minutes or until golden brown. Refrigerate leftovers.

★★★★

FISHERMAN'S PIE

Makes 6 servings

1½ cups biscuit baking mix
6 tablespoons water
1 pound white fish fillets, fresh
  or frozen, thawed, cut into
  small pieces
1 (15-ounce) can Snow's® or
  Doxsee® Condensed New
  England Clam Chowder
1 (6½-ounce) can Snow's® or
  Doxsee® Minced or Chopped
  Clams, drained
⅓ cup Borden® or Meadow Gold®
  Half-and-Half or Milk
1 medium tomato, seeded and
  chopped
¼ cup chopped green bell pepper
3 tablespoons flour
1 teaspoon thyme leaves
⅛ to ¼ teaspoon pepper
1 egg, beaten, optional

Preheat oven to 400°. In small bowl, combine biscuit mix and water; mix well. On floured surface, roll out dough to circle 1 inch larger than 1½-quart round baking dish; make slits or cut-outs in center. In medium saucepan, combine remaining ingredients except egg; heat through. Pour into baking dish. Top with dough; turn under edge, seal and flute. Brush with egg if desired. Bake 25 to 30 minutes or until golden brown. Let stand 10 minutes before serving. Refrigerate leftovers.

★ ★ ★ ★

MEXICAN PAN PIZZA

Makes 8 to 10 servings

2½ cups biscuit baking mix
½ cup yellow cornmeal
½ cup water
¼ cup margarine or butter, melted
1 pound lean ground beef
½ cup chopped onion
1 (8-ounce) can tomato sauce
1 (4-ounce) can chopped green
    chilies, drained
2 teaspoons Wyler's® or Steero®
    Beef-Flavor Instant Bouillon
    or 2 Beef-Flavor Bouillon
    Cubes
1 teaspoon chili powder
¼ teaspoon ground cumin
1 (16-ounce) can refried beans
1½ cups (6 ounces) shredded Colby
    or Monterey Jack cheese
    Chopped tomatoes, shredded
    lettuce and sliced pitted ripe
    olives

Preheat oven to 425°. In medium bowl, combine biscuit mix, cornmeal, water and margarine; mix well. Pat dough on bottom and up sides of greased 15×10-inch jellyroll pan. Bake 10 minutes; remove from oven. Meanwhile, in large skillet, brown meat with onion; stir in tomato sauce, chilies, bouillon, chili powder and cumin. Cook and stir until bouillon dissolves. Spread beans evenly over baked crust; spoon meat mixture evenly over beans. Top with cheese. Bake 10 minutes. Garnish with tomato, lettuce and olives. Refrigerate leftovers.

★★★★
COUNTRY SAUSAGE QUICHE

Makes one 9-inch quiche

1 (9-inch) unbaked pastry shell
½ pound bulk country sausage
½ cup chopped onion
1 (8-ounce) container Borden® or Meadow Gold® Sour Cream, at room temperature
3 eggs
2 tablespoons flour
2 teaspoons Wyler's® or Steero® Chicken- *or* Beef-Flavor Instant Bouillon
1½ cups (6 ounces) shredded Swiss cheese
1 cup frozen green peas, thawed
1 (2½-ounce) jar sliced mushrooms, drained
1 (2-ounce) jar pimientos, drained and chopped
⅛ teaspoon ground nutmeg

Preheat oven to 450°. Bake pastry shell 8 minutes; remove from oven. Reduce oven temperature to 350°. Meanwhile, in medium skillet, cook sausage and onion; pour off fat. In large bowl, beat sour cream, eggs, flour and bouillon. Stir in remaining ingredients. Turn into prepared pastry shell. Bake 40 minutes or until set. Let stand 10 minutes before serving. Refrigerate leftovers.

★★★★
CHEEZY TAMALE PIE

Makes one 9-inch pie

Pie crust mix for one 9-inch pastry shell (about 1 cup mix)
¼ cup cornmeal
¼ cup cold water
½ pound lean ground beef
½ cup chopped onion
3 tablespoons flour
1 (15-ounce) can kidney beans, drained
1 (8-ounce) can tomato sauce
2 teaspoons chili powder
1 cup Fisher® Ched-O-Mate® Shredded Cheddar Cheese Substitute
1 cup shredded lettuce
½ cup chopped fresh tomato

Preheat oven to 400°. In medium bowl, combine pie crust mix and cornmeal. Stir in water to form dough; roll out to fit 9-inch pie plate. Line pie plate with dough; flute edge. Prick bottom and side thoroughly with fork. Bake 8 minutes; remove from oven. Meanwhile, in large skillet, brown meat with onion; pour off fat. Stir in flour. Add beans, sauce, chili powder and cheese substitute; mix well. Spoon into prepared pastry shell. Bake 20 minutes or until hot and bubbly. Let stand 15 minutes before serving. Top with lettuce and tomato. Refrigerate leftovers.

★ ★ ★ ★
SWISS CHICKEN
QUICHE

Makes one 9-inch quiche

1 (9-inch) unbaked pastry shell
2 cups cubed cooked chicken or
   turkey
1 cup (4 ounces) shredded Swiss
   cheese
2 tablespoons flour
1 tablespoon Wyler's® or Steero®
   Chicken-Flavor Instant
   Bouillon
1 cup Borden® or Meadow Gold®
   Milk
3 eggs, beaten
¼ cup chopped onion
2 tablespoons chopped green bell
   pepper
2 tablespoons chopped pimiento

Preheat oven to 425°. Bake pastry shell 8 minutes; remove from oven. Reduce oven temperature to 350°. Meanwhile, in medium bowl, toss cheese with flour and bouillon; add remaining ingredients. Mix well. Pour into prepared pastry shell. Bake 40 to 45 minutes or until set. Let stand 10 minutes before serving. Garnish as desired. Refrigerate leftovers.

★★★★
DOWNEAST CLAM PIE

Makes one 9-inch pie

Pastry for 2-crust pie
3 slices bacon
¼ cup chopped onion
¼ cup unsifted flour
1 (15-ounce) can Snow's® or
   Doxsee® Condensed New
   England Clam Chowder
1 (6½-ounce) can Snow's® or
   Doxsee® Chopped or Minced
   Clams, drained, reserving
   ¼ cup liquid
½ cup Borden® or Meadow Gold®
   Coffee Cream or Half-and-
   Half
2 tablespoons chopped fresh
   parsley
1 egg, beaten

Place rack in lowest position in oven; preheat oven to 425°. In medium skillet, cook bacon until crisp; remove and crumble. In 2 tablespoons drippings, cook onion until tender; stir in flour until smooth. Gradually stir in chowder, reserved clam liquid and cream; cook and stir until thickened. Stir in clams, bacon and parsley. Turn into pastry-lined 9-inch pie plate. Cover with top crust; cut slits near center. Seal and flute; brush with egg. Bake 30 minutes or until golden. Let stand 20 minutes before serving. Garnish as desired. Refrigerate leftovers.

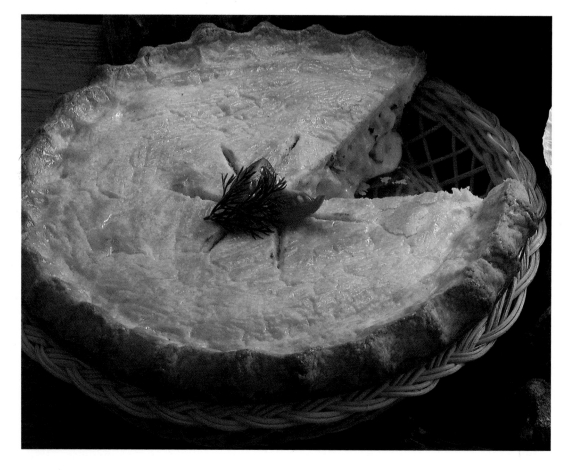

★★★★
CALICO BROCCOLI QUICHE

Makes one 9-inch quiche

1 (9-inch) unbaked pastry shell
1 (10-ounce) package frozen
    chopped broccoli or spinach,
    thawed and *well drained*
½ cup shredded carrot
¼ cup chopped onion
2 tablespoons margarine or butter
3 eggs
1 cup Borden® or Meadow Gold®
    Half-and-Half or Milk
1 tablespoon Wyler's® or Steero®
    Chicken-Flavor Instant
    Bouillon
⅛ to ¼ teaspoon ground nutmeg
1½ cups (6 ounces) shredded Swiss
    or cheddar cheese
1 tablespoon flour

Preheat oven to 425°. Bake pastry shell
8 minutes; remove from oven. Reduce
oven temperature to 350°. Meanwhile,
in small saucepan, cook carrot and
onion in margarine until tender. In
medium bowl, beat eggs, half-and-half,
bouillon and nutmeg. Toss together
cheese and flour; add to egg mixture
along with remaining ingredients.
Turn into prepared pastry shell. Bake
40 minutes or until set. Let stand
10 minutes before serving. Garnish
as desired. Refrigerate leftovers.

Mini Meat Pies

★★★★
MINI MEAT PIES

Makes about 40 appetizers

½ pound lean ground beef,
    browned and drained
2 hard-cooked eggs, finely
    chopped
¼ cup Borden® or Meadow Gold®
    Sour Cream
1 tablespoon chopped parsley
1 teaspoon Wyler's® or Steero®
    Beef-Flavor Instant Bouillon
1 (11-ounce) package pie crust mix

Preheat oven to 400°. In medium
bowl, combine all ingredients except
pie crust mix; mix well. Prepare pie
crust mix as package directs. Divide
dough in half. On floured surface, roll
out half the dough to 10×13-inch
rectangle, ⅛-inch thick; cut into 20
(2½-inch) squares. Spoon 1 heaping
teaspoon meat mixture in center of
each square; fold as desired. Repeat
with remaining dough and meat
mixture. Place 1 inch apart on
ungreased baking sheets. Bake 12 to 15
minutes or until lightly browned.
Serve hot. Refrigerate leftovers.

Crab & Shrimp Quiche

★ ★ ★ ★

CRAB & SHRIMP QUICHE

Makes one 9-inch quiche

1 (9-inch) unbaked pastry shell
6 slices Borden® Process
    American Cheese Food
2 tablespoons sliced green onion
2 tablespoons chopped pimiento
1 tablespoon flour
1 (6-ounce) can Orleans® or
    Harris® Crabmeat, drained
1 (4¼-ounce) can Orleans®
    Shrimp, drained and soaked
    as label directs
1½ cups Borden® or Meadow Gold®
    Half-and-Half
3 eggs, beaten

Place rack in lowest position in oven; preheat oven to 425°. Cut *4 slices* cheese food into pieces. In large bowl, toss cheese food pieces, onion and pimiento with flour. Add remaining ingredients except pastry shell and cheese food slices. Pour into pastry shell. Bake 20 minutes. Reduce oven temperature to 325°; bake 20 minutes longer or until set. Arrange remaining *2 slices* cheese food on top of quiche. Let stand 10 minutes before serving. Garnish as desired. Refrigerate leftovers.

★ ★ ★ ★

CHEESY VEGETABLE "UN-QUICHE"

Makes 6 servings; 156 calories per serving

1 (10-ounce) package frozen
    chopped broccoli or spinach,
    thawed and *well drained*
¼ cup chopped onion
1 clove garlic, finely chopped
1 tablespoon diet margarine
8 slices Borden® Lite-line®
    Process Cheese Product, any
    flavor, cut into small pieces*
3 tablespoons flour
3 eggs, beaten
1 cup Borden® Lite-line® or
    Viva® Skim Milk
⅛ to ¼ teaspoon ground nutmeg
½ cup shredded carrot

Preheat oven to 350°. In small saucepan, cook onion and garlic in margarine until tender. In medium bowl, toss cheese product pieces with flour; add eggs, milk and nutmeg. Mix well. Add broccoli, onion and carrot. Pour into lightly oiled 9-inch pie plate. Bake 40 to 45 minutes or until set and golden brown. Let stand 10 minutes before serving. Refrigerate leftovers.

*½ calories of process cheese—8% milkfat version

★ ★ ★ ★
TEX-MEX TACO PIE

Makes one 9-inch pie

Cornmeal Crust
1 pound lean ground beef
½ cup chopped onion
1 (8-ounce) can tomato sauce
1 (4-ounce) can chopped green
  chilies, drained
2 teaspoons Wyler's® or Steero®
  Beef-Flavor Instant Bouillon
1¼ teaspoons chili powder
¼ teaspoon ground cumin
1 egg, beaten

Preheat oven to 350°. Prepare Cornmeal Crust. In large skillet, brown meat with onion; pour off fat. Add tomato sauce, chilies, bouillon, chili powder and cumin; cook and stir until bouillon dissolves. Remove from heat; stir in egg. Spoon into prepared crust. Bake 25 minutes or until hot. Let stand 5 minutes. Garnish as desired. Refrigerate leftovers.

CORNMEAL CRUST: In medium bowl, combine 1 cup biscuit baking mix, 3 tablespoons cornmeal, 3 tablespoons margarine or butter, melted, and 2 tablespoons water; mix well. Press on bottom and up side of 9-inch pie plate. Flute if desired.

AKED ★ PIES

★★★★

Apple, pumpkin,
pecan, custard, peach
and cherry—here
you'll find delicious
new twists to these
popular American pies.
And tempt any pie
lover with rich Fudge
Brownie, Cranberry
Mince and Lemon
Sponge pies warm
from the oven.

★★★★

Pictured here is Harvest Fruit
Custard Tart; see page 24 for recipe.

═══════ ★★★★ ═══════

HARVEST FRUIT CUSTARD TART

Makes one 9- or 10-inch pie

  1 (9- or 10-inch) unbaked pastry shell
1½ cups Borden® or Meadow Gold® Sour Cream
  1 (14-ounce) can Eagle® Brand Sweetened Condensed Milk (NOT evaporated milk)
  ¼ cup frozen apple juice concentrate, thawed
  1 egg
1½ teaspoons vanilla extract
  ¼ teaspoon ground cinnamon
  ¾ pound all-purpose apples or pears, cored, pared and thinly sliced (about 2 cups)
  1 tablespoon margarine or butter
    Cinnamon Glaze

Preheat oven to 375°. Bake pastry shell 15 minutes. Meanwhile, in large mixer bowl, beat sour cream, sweetened condensed milk, juice concentrate, egg, vanilla and cinnamon; pour into prepared pastry shell. Bake 30 minutes or until set. Cool. In skillet, cook apples in margarine until tender-crisp. Arrange on pie; drizzle with Cinnamon Glaze. Refrigerate leftovers.

CINNAMON GLAZE: In small saucepan, mix ¼ cup thawed frozen apple juice concentrate, 1 teaspoon cornstarch and ¼ teaspoon ground cinnamon; cook and stir until thickened. (Makes about ¼ cup)

═══════ ★★★★ ═══════

PUMPKIN MINCEMEAT PIE

Makes one 9- or 10-inch pie

  1 (9- or 10-inch) unbaked pastry shell
  1 (9-ounce) package None Such® Condensed Mincemeat, crumbled
  ¾ cup water
  1 (16-ounce) can pumpkin (2 cups)
  1 (14-ounce) can Eagle® Brand Sweetened Condensed Milk (NOT evaporated milk)
  2 eggs
  1 teaspoon ground cinnamon
  ½ teaspoon ground ginger
  ½ teaspoon ground nutmeg
  ½ teaspoon salt

Place rack in lowest position in oven; preheat oven to 425°. In small saucepan, combine mincemeat and water; bring to a boil. Cook and stir 1 minute. Turn into pastry shell. In large mixer bowl, combine remaining ingredients; mix well. Pour over mincemeat. Bake 15 minutes. Reduce oven temperature to 350°; bake 35 to 40 minutes longer or until set in center. Cool. Serve warm or chilled. Refrigerate leftovers.

TIP: 1⅓ cups (one-half jar) None Such® Ready-to-Use Mincemeat (Regular *or* Brandy & Rum) can be substituted for None Such® Condensed Mincemeat.

===★ ★ ★ ★===

MOCHA WALNUT TART

Makes one 9-inch pie

1 (9-inch) unbaked pastry shell
2 (1-ounce) squares unsweetened
  chocolate
¼ cup margarine or butter
1 (14-ounce) can Eagle® Brand
  Sweetened Condensed Milk
  (NOT evaporated milk)
¼ cup water
2 eggs, well beaten
¼ cup coffee-flavored liqueur
1 teaspoon vanilla extract
⅛ teaspoon salt
1 cup walnuts, toasted and
  chopped

Preheat oven to 350°. In medium saucepan, over low heat, melt chocolate and margarine. Stir in sweetened condensed milk, water and eggs; *mix well.* Remove from heat; stir in liqueur, vanilla and salt. Pour into pastry shell; top with walnuts. Bake 40 to 45 minutes or until center is set. Cool. Serve warm or chilled. Garnish as desired. Refrigerate leftovers.

Deep-Dish Pumpkin Pie

★★★★
DEEP-DISH PUMPKIN PIE

Makes 8 to 10 servings

1¾ cups unsifted flour
⅓ cup firmly packed brown sugar
⅓ cup granulated sugar
1 cup cold margarine or butter, cut into small pieces
1 cup chopped nuts
1 (16-ounce) can pumpkin (2 cups)
1 (14-ounce) can Eagle® Brand Sweetened Condensed Milk (NOT evaporated milk)
2 eggs
1 teaspoon ground cinnamon
½ teaspoon ground allspice
½ teaspoon salt

Preheat oven to 350°. In medium bowl, combine flour and sugars; cut in margarine until crumbly. Stir in nuts. Reserving 1 cup crumb mixture, press remainder firmly on bottom and halfway up sides of 12×7-inch baking dish. In large mixer bowl, combine remaining ingredients except reserved crumb mixture; mix well. Pour into prepared dish. Top with reserved crumb mixture. Bake 55 minutes or until golden. Cool. Serve with ice cream if desired. Refrigerate leftovers.

★★★★
CITRUS CHESS PIE

Makes one 9-inch pie

1 (9-inch) unbaked pastry shell
1 cup fresh bread crumbs (2 slices)
¼ cup Borden® or Meadow Gold® Milk
1¼ cups sugar
¼ cup margarine or butter, melted
4 eggs
⅓ cup orange juice
⅓ cup ReaLemon® Lemon Juice from Concentrate

Preheat oven to 425°. Bake pastry shell 8 minutes; remove from oven. Reduce oven temperature to 350°. Meanwhile, in large mixer bowl, combine crumbs and milk; let stand 5 minutes. Add remaining ingredients; beat well. Pour into prepared pastry shell; bake 40 to 45 minutes or until knife inserted near center comes out clean. Cool. Refrigerate leftovers.

★★★★
MAPLE PECAN PIE

Makes one 9-inch pie

1 (9-inch) unbaked pastry shell
3 eggs, beaten
1 cup Cary's®, Vermont Maple
    Orchards or MacDonald's
    Pure Maple Syrup
½ cup firmly packed light brown
    sugar
2 tablespoons butter or
    margarine, melted
1 teaspoon vanilla extract
1¼ cups pecan halves or pieces

Place rack in lowest position in oven;
preheat oven to 350°. In medium
bowl, combine all ingredients except
pastry shell. Pour into pastry shell.
Bake 35 to 40 minutes or until golden.
Cool. Chill if desired. Refrigerate
leftovers.

★★★★
OLD-FASHIONED BUTTERMILK PIE

Makes one 9-inch pie

1 (9-inch) unbaked pastry shell
3 eggs
1¼ cups sugar
3 tablespoons flour
¼ teaspoon ground nutmeg
1 cup Borden® or Meadow Gold®
    Buttermilk
⅓ cup butter or margarine, melted
1 teaspoon vanilla extract

Preheat oven to 400°. In large mixer
bowl, beat eggs. Add sugar, flour and
nutmeg; mix well. Beat in remaining
ingredients except pastry shell. Pour
into pastry shell. Bake 10 minutes.
Reduce oven temperature to 325°;
bake 35 minutes longer or until knife
inserted near edge comes out clean.
Cool. Serve with fresh fruit if desired.
Refrigerate leftovers.

Maple Pecan Pie

★★★★
PEACH AMARETTO CHEESE PIE

Makes one 9-inch pie

1 (9-inch) unbaked pastry shell
1 (8-ounce) package cream cheese, softened
1 (14-ounce) can Eagle® Brand Sweetened Condensed Milk (NOT evaporated milk)
2 eggs
3 tablespoons amaretto liqueur
1½ teaspoons almond extract
3 medium peaches, seeded, peeled and sliced, *or* 1 (16-ounce) package frozen peach slices, thawed and well drained
2 tablespoons Bama® Peach Preserves

Preheat oven to 375°. Bake pastry shell 15 minutes. Meanwhile, in large mixer bowl, beat cheese until fluffy. Gradually beat in sweetened condensed milk until smooth. Add eggs, *2 tablespoons* amaretto and *1 teaspoon* extract; mix well. Pour into prepared pastry shell. Bake 25 minutes or until set. Cool. Arrange peach slices on top of pie. In small saucepan, combine preserves, remaining *1 tablespoon* amaretto and remaining *½ teaspoon* extract; over low heat, cook and stir until hot. Spoon over top of pie. Chill. Garnish as desired. Refrigerate leftovers.

★★★★
BLUEBERRY STREUSEL COBBLER

Makes 8 to 12 servings

1 pint fresh or frozen blueberries,
   rinsed and sorted
1 (14-ounce) can Eagle® Brand
   Sweetened Condensed Milk
   (NOT evaporated milk)
2 teaspoons grated lemon rind
¾ cup plus 2 tablespoons cold
   margarine or butter
2 cups biscuit baking mix
½ cup firmly packed brown sugar
½ cup chopped nuts
   Blueberry Sauce

Preheat oven to 325°. In medium
bowl, combine blueberries, sweetened
condensed milk and rind. In large
bowl, cut *¾ cup* margarine into *1½
cups* biscuit mix until crumbly; add
blueberry mixture. Spread in greased
9-inch square baking pan. In small
bowl, combine remaining *½ cup*
biscuit mix and sugar; cut in remaining
2 tablespoons margarine until crumbly.
Add nuts. Sprinkle over cobbler.
Bake 1 hour and 10 minutes or until
golden. Serve warm with vanilla
ice cream and Blueberry Sauce.
Refrigerate leftovers.

BLUEBERRY SAUCE: In small
saucepan, combine ½ cup granulated
sugar, 1 tablespoon cornstarch,
½ teaspoon ground cinnamon and
¼ teaspoon ground nutmeg.
Gradually add ½ cup water. Cook and
stir until thickened. Stir in 1 pint
blueberries; cook and stir until hot.
(Makes about 1⅔ cups)

Blueberry Streusel Cobbler

★★★★
CHOCOLATE MINCE PECAN PIE

Makes one 9-inch pie

1 (9-inch) unbaked pastry shell
½ cup sugar
2 tablespoons flour
1 egg, beaten
1 jar None Such® Ready-to-Use
   Mincemeat (Regular *or*
   Brandy & Rum)
1 cup chopped pecans
3 (1-ounce) squares semi-sweet *or*
   unsweetened chocolate,
   melted
2 tablespoons margarine or
   butter, melted

Place rack in lowest position in oven;
preheat oven to 400°. In large bowl,
combine sugar and flour. Add egg;
mix well. Add mincemeat, pecans,
chocolate and margarine; mix well.
Turn into pastry shell. Bake 15
minutes. Reduce oven temperature to
325°; bake 50 minutes longer or until
filling is slightly puffed and firm. Cool
slightly. Serve warm or cooled.

Lemon Sponge Pie

★★★★

LEMON SPONGE PIE

Makes one 9-inch pie

1 (9-inch) unbaked pastry shell
3 eggs, separated
1 (14-ounce) can Eagle® Brand
    Sweetened Condensed Milk
    (NOT evaporated milk)
⅓ cup ReaLemon® Lemon Juice
    from Concentrate
2 tablespoons flour
2 teaspoons grated lemon rind
    Yellow food coloring, optional

Preheat oven to 375°. Bake pastry shell 10 minutes; remove from oven. Reduce oven temperature to 350°. In large mixer bowl, combine remaining ingredients except egg whites; mix well. In small mixer bowl, beat egg whites until stiff but not dry; fold into lemon mixture. Pour into prepared pastry shell. Bake 25 minutes or until set. Cool. Serve warm or chilled. Garnish as desired. Refrigerate leftovers.

★★★★

APPLE MINCE PIE

Makes one 9-inch pie

Pastry for 2-crust pie
1 pound all-purpose apples,
    cored, pared and thinly sliced
    (about 3 cups)
3 tablespoons flour
2 tablespoons margarine or
    butter, melted
1 jar None Such® Ready-to-Use
    Mincemeat (Regular *or*
    Brandy & Rum)
1 egg yolk plus 2 tablespoons
    water, optional

Place rack in lowest position in oven; preheat oven to 425°. In large bowl, toss apples with flour and margarine; arrange in pastry-lined 9-inch pie plate. Top with mincemeat. Cover with top crust; cut slits near center. Seal and flute. For a more golden crust, mix egg yolk and water; brush over entire surface of pie. Bake 10 minutes. Reduce oven temperature to 375°; bake 25 minutes longer or until golden. Cool. Garnish as desired.

TIP: 1 (9-ounce) package None Such® Condensed Mincemeat, reconstituted as package directs, can be substituted for None Such® Ready-to-Use Mincemeat.

Apple Mince Pie

★★★★
TRADITIONAL PUMPKIN PIE

Makes one 9-inch pie

1 (9-inch) unbaked pastry shell
1 (16-ounce) can pumpkin
    (2 cups)
1 (14-ounce) can Eagle® Brand
    Sweetened Condensed Milk
    (NOT evaporated milk)
2 eggs
1 teaspoon ground cinnamon
½ teaspoon ground ginger
½ teaspoon ground nutmeg
½ teaspoon salt

Place rack in lowest position in oven; preheat oven to 425°. In large mixer bowl, combine all ingredients except pastry shell; mix well. Pour into pastry shell. Bake 15 minutes. Reduce oven temperature to 350°; bake 35 to 40 minutes longer or until knife inserted near edge comes out clean. Cool. Garnish as desired. Refrigerate leftovers.

OPTIONAL TOPPINGS

Sour Cream Topping: In medium bowl, combine 1½ cups Borden® or Meadow Gold® Sour Cream, 2 tablespoons sugar and 1 teaspoon vanilla extract. After 30 minutes of baking, spread evenly over top of pie; bake 10 minutes longer. Garnish as desired.

Streusel Topping: In medium bowl, combine ½ cup firmly packed light brown sugar and ½ cup unsifted flour; cut in ¼ cup cold margarine or butter until crumbly. Stir in ¼ cup chopped nuts. After 30 minutes of baking, sprinkle on top of pic; bake 10 minutes longer.

Traditional Pumpkin Pie

★★★★
SPIRITED EGG NOG CUSTARD PIE

Makes one 9-inch pie

1 (9-inch) unbaked pastry shell
1 (14-ounce) can Eagle® Brand
    Sweetened Condensed Milk
    (NOT evaporated milk)
1⅓ cups water
2 tablespoons light rum
1 tablespoon brandy
1 teaspoon vanilla extract
½ teaspoon ground nutmeg
3 eggs, beaten

Preheat oven to 425°. Bake pastry shell 8 minutes. Meanwhile, in large bowl, combine all ingredients except eggs; mix well. Add eggs. Pour into prepared pastry shell. Bake 10 minutes. Reduce oven temperature to 325°; bake 25 minutes longer or until knife inserted near center comes out clean. Cool. Chill if desired. Refrigerate leftovers.

★★★★

CRANBERRY CRUMB PIE

Makes one 9-inch pie

1 (9-inch) unbaked pastry shell
1 (8-ounce) package cream cheese, softened
1 (14-ounce) can Eagle® Brand Sweetened Condensed Milk (NOT evaporated milk)
¼ cup ReaLemon® Lemon Juice from Concentrate
3 tablespoons light brown sugar
2 tablespoons cornstarch
1 (16-ounce) can whole berry cranberry sauce
¼ cup cold margarine or butter
⅓ cup unsifted flour
¾ cup chopped walnuts

Preheat oven to 425°. Bake pastry shell 8 minutes; remove from oven. Reduce oven temperature to 375°. Meanwhile, in large mixer bowl, beat cheese until fluffy. Gradually beat in sweetened condensed milk until smooth. Stir in ReaLemon® brand. Pour into prepared pastry shell. In small bowl, combine *1 tablespoon* sugar and cornstarch; mix well. Stir in cranberry sauce. Spoon evenly over cheese mixture. In medium bowl, cut margarine into flour and remaining *2 tablespoons* sugar until crumbly. Stir in nuts. Sprinkle evenly over cranberry mixture. Bake 45 to 50 minutes or until bubbly and golden. Cool. Serve at room temperature or chill. Refrigerate leftovers.

★ ★ ★ ★

DEEP-DISH
APPLE-COT PIE

Makes 8 to 10 servings

Pastry for 1-crust pie
3 pounds all-purpose apples,
    cored, pared and sliced (about
    8 cups)
1 tablespoon ReaLemon® Lemon
    Juice from Concentrate
½ cup unsifted flour
½ to ¾ cup sugar
1½ teaspoons ground cinnamon
1 teaspoon ground nutmeg
1 (16-ounce) jar Bama® Apricot
    or Peach Preserves
1 egg yolk plus 2 tablespoons
    water, optional

Preheat oven to 375°. In large bowl, sprinkle apples with ReaLemon® brand. Combine flour, sugar, cinnamon and nutmeg; toss with apples. Add preserves; mix well. Turn into well-buttered 12×7-inch baking dish. Roll pastry 1½ inches larger than baking dish; cut slits near center. Place pastry over apples; turn under edges, seal and flute. For a more golden crust, mix egg yolk and water; brush over entire surface of pie. Bake 40 to 45 minutes or until golden brown. Serve warm with ice cream if desired.

Orange Blossom Pie

ORANGE BLOSSOM PIE

Makes one 9-inch pie

1 (9-inch) unbaked pastry shell
1 (14-ounce) can Eagle® Brand Sweetened Condensed Milk (NOT evaporated milk)
1 cup orange juice
2 egg yolks
1 tablespoon grated orange rind
1 (3-ounce) package cream cheese, softened
½ cup Borden® or Meadow Gold® Sour Cream, at room temperature
½ cup confectioners' sugar
½ teaspoon vanilla extract

Preheat oven to 375°. Bake pastry shell 15 minutes. Remove from oven; reduce oven temperature to 325°. Meanwhile, in large bowl, combine sweetened condensed milk, orange juice, egg yolks and rind; mix well. Pour into prepared pastry shell (mixture will be thin). Bake 35 minutes or until set. Meanwhile, in small mixer bowl, beat remaining ingredients until smooth; spread over pie. Bake 5 minutes longer. Cool. Chill. Garnish as desired. Refrigerate leftovers.

NEW ENGLAND MAPLE APPLE PIE

Makes one 9-inch pie

1 (9-inch) unbaked pastry shell
2 pounds all-purpose apples, cored, pared and thinly sliced (about 6 cups)
½ cup plus 2 tablespoons unsifted flour
½ cup Cary's®, Vermont Maple Orchards or MacDonald's Pure Maple Syrup
2 tablespoons margarine or butter, melted
¼ cup firmly packed light brown sugar
1 teaspoon ground cinnamon
⅓ cup cold margarine or butter
½ cup chopped nuts

Place rack in lowest position in oven; preheat oven to 400°. In large bowl, combine apples and *2 tablespoons* flour. Combine syrup and melted margarine. Pour over apples; mix well. Turn into pastry shell. In medium bowl, combine remaining *½ cup* flour, sugar and cinnamon; cut in cold margarine until crumbly. Add nuts; sprinkle over apples. Bake 10 minutes. Reduce oven temperature to 375°; bake 35 minutes longer or until golden brown. Cool slightly. Serve warm.

★★★★
APPLE BUTTER YAM PIE

Makes one 9-inch pie

1 (9-inch) unbaked pastry shell
1 cup hot mashed yams or sweet
    potatoes (about ¾ pound raw)
½ cup margarine or butter,
    softened
½ cup firmly packed light brown
    sugar
2 tablespoons flour
1 (15-ounce) jar Bama® Apple
    Butter
½ cup Borden® or Meadow Gold®
    Milk
1½ teaspoons grated orange rind
¼ teaspoon salt
3 eggs
    Whipped cream and nuts,
    optional

Preheat oven to 400°. In large mixer bowl, beat yams, margarine, sugar and flour until well blended. Add apple butter, milk, rind, salt and eggs; beat well. Turn into pastry shell. Bake 10 minutes. Reduce oven temperature to 350°; bake 50 minutes longer or until knife inserted near edge comes out clean. Cool. Serve warm or chilled. Garnish with whipped cream and nuts if desired. Refrigerate leftovers.

TIP: Canned yams can be substituted for fresh yams; melt margarine. Proceed as above.

★★★★
APPLESAUCE SPICE PIE

Makes one 9-inch pie

1 (9-inch) unbaked pastry shell
1 (16-ounce) jar applesauce
¾ cup firmly packed light brown
   sugar
4 eggs
¼ cup ReaLemon® Lemon Juice
   from Concentrate
2 tablespoons margarine or
   butter, melted
1 tablespoon flour
¾ teaspoon salt
½ teaspoon ground cinnamon
¼ teaspoon ground nutmeg

Preheat oven to 425°. In large mixer bowl, combine all ingredients except pastry shell; mix well. Pour into pastry shell. Bake 15 minutes. Reduce oven temperature to 325°; bake 30 minutes longer or until wooden pick inserted near edge comes out clean. Cool. Serve warm with ice cream or whipped cream if desired. Refrigerate leftovers.

★★★★
MINCE ALMOND PIE

Makes one 9-inch pie

1 (9-inch) unbaked pastry shell
1 jar None Such® Ready-to-Use
   Regular Mincemeat
¼ cup amaretto liqueur
¾ cup sliced almonds

Place rack in lowest position in oven; preheat oven to 400°. In medium bowl, combine mincemeat and amaretto; turn into pastry shell. Top with almonds. Bake 25 minutes or until bubbly. Cool. Serve warm or cooled.

★★★★
DEEP-DISH PEACH PIE

Makes one 8-inch pie

Pastry for 1-crust pie
1 cup plus 1 tablespoon sugar
2 tablespoons cornstarch
3 pounds peaches, seeded, pared
   and sliced (about 6 cups)
2 tablespoons ReaLemon® Lemon
   Juice from Concentrate
2 tablespoons margarine or
   butter, melted
¼ teaspoon almond extract
1 egg yolk plus 2 tablespoons
   water
2 tablespoons sliced almonds

Preheat oven to 375°. In small bowl, combine *1 cup* sugar and cornstarch. In large bowl, toss peaches with ReaLemon® brand; add sugar mixture, margarine and extract. Turn into 8-inch square baking dish. Roll pastry to 9-inch square; cut slits near center. Place pastry over filling; turn under edges, seal and flute. Mix egg yolk and water; brush over entire surface of pie. Sprinkle with remaining *1 tablespoon* sugar and almonds. Bake 45 to 50 minutes or until golden brown.

CANNED PEACH PIE: Omit fresh peaches. Reserving ½ cup syrup, drain 2 (29-ounce) cans peach slices. Combine sugar and cornstarch as above. Toss peaches with ReaLemon® brand and reserved syrup; stir in sugar mixture, margarine and extract. Proceed as above.

Deep-Dish Peach Pie

Sweet Potato Pecan Pie

★ ★ ★ ★
WALNUT MINCE PIE

Makes one 9-inch pie

1 (9-inch) unbaked pastry shell
½ cup sugar
2 tablespoons flour
⅛ teaspoon salt
2 eggs
2 tablespoons margarine or
    butter, melted
1 cup chopped walnuts
1 jar None Such® Ready-to-Use
    Mincemeat (Regular *or*
    Brandy & Rum)

Preheat oven to 400°. In large bowl, combine sugar, flour and salt. Add eggs; mix well. Add margarine, walnuts and mincemeat; mix well. Turn into pastry shell. Bake 15 minutes. Reduce oven temperature to 325°; bake 50 minutes longer or until filling is slightly puffed and firm. Cool slightly. Serve warm or cooled. Refrigerate leftovers.

PECAN MINCE PIE: Substitute chopped pecans for walnuts; proceed as above.

★ ★ ★ ★
SWEET POTATO PECAN PIE

Makes one 9-inch pie

1 (9-inch) unbaked pastry shell
1 pound (2 medium) yams or
    sweet potatoes, cooked and
    peeled
¼ cup margarine or butter
1 (14-ounce) can Eagle® Brand
    Sweetened Condensed Milk
    (NOT evaporated milk)
1 teaspoon grated orange rind
1 teaspoon vanilla extract
1 teaspoon ground cinnamon
½ teaspoon ground nutmeg
¼ teaspoon salt
2 eggs
    Pecan Topping

Preheat oven to 350°. In large mixer bowl, beat *hot* yams with margarine until smooth. Add remaining ingredients except pastry shell and Pecan Topping; mix well. Pour into pastry shell. Bake 30 minutes. Remove from oven; spoon Pecan Topping evenly over top. Bake 20 to 25 minutes longer or until golden brown. Cool. Serve warm or chilled. Garnish as desired. Refrigerate leftovers.

PECAN TOPPING: In small mixer bowl, combine 1 egg, 3 tablespoons dark corn syrup, 3 tablespoons light brown sugar, 1 tablespoon margarine or butter, melted, and ½ teaspoon maple flavoring; mix well. Stir in 1 cup chopped pecans.

★★★★
HARVEST CHERRY PIE

Makes one 9-inch pie

Pastry for 2-crust pie
1 (9-ounce) package None Such® Condensed Mincemeat
¾ cup chopped nuts
1 (21-ounce) can cherry pie filling
1 egg yolk plus 2 tablespoons water, optional

Place rack in lowest position in oven; preheat oven to 425°. Reconstitute mincemeat as package directs; stir in nuts. Turn into pastry-lined 9-inch pie plate. Spoon cherry pie filling over mincemeat. Cover with top crust; cut slits near center. Seal and flute. For a more golden crust, mix egg yolk and water; brush over entire surface of pie. Bake 25 to 30 minutes or until golden brown. Serve warm or cooled. Garnish as desired.

TIP: One-half jar None Such® Ready-to-Use Mincemeat (Regular *or* Brandy & Rum) can be substituted for None Such® Condensed Mincemeat.

Harvest Cherry Pie

Fudge Brownie Pie

★★★★
FUDGE BROWNIE PIE

Makes one 9-inch pie

1 (9-inch) unbaked pastry shell
1 (6-ounce) package semi-sweet chocolate chips (1 cup)
¼ cup margarine or butter
1 (14-ounce) can Eagle® Brand Sweetened Condensed Milk (NOT evaporated milk)
½ cup biscuit baking mix
2 eggs
1 teaspoon vanilla extract
1 cup chopped nuts

Preheat oven to 375°. Bake pastry shell 10 minutes; remove from oven. Reduce oven temperature to 325°. Meanwhile in saucepan, over low heat, melt chips with margarine. In large mixer bowl, beat chocolate mixture with remaining ingredients except nuts until smooth. Add nuts. Pour into prepared pastry shell. Bake 35 to 40 minutes or until center is set. Cool slightly. Serve with ice cream if desired. Refrigerate leftovers.

Cranberry Mince Pie

CRANBERRY MINCE PIE

Makes one 9- or 10-inch pie

   Pastry for 2-crust pie
⅔ cup sugar
 2 tablespoons cornstarch
⅔ cup water
1½ cups fresh or dry-pack frozen
     cranberries, rinsed and sorted
 1 jar None Such® Ready-to-Use
     Mincemeat (Regular *or*
     Brandy & Rum)
 1 egg yolk plus 2 tablespoons
     water, optional

Place rack in lowest position in oven; preheat oven to 425°. In medium saucepan, combine sugar and cornstarch; stir in water. Over high heat, cook and stir until boiling. Add cranberries; return to a boil. Reduce heat; simmer 5 to 10 minutes, stirring occasionally. Turn mincemeat into pastry-lined 9- or 10-inch pie plate. Top with cranberries. Cover with top crust; cut slits near center. Seal and flute. For a more golden crust, mix egg yolk and water; brush over entire surface of pie. Bake 30 minutes or until golden. Cool. Garnish as desired.

TIP: Omit sugar, cornstarch, water and cranberries. Spoon 1 (16-ounce) can whole berry cranberry sauce evenly over mincemeat. Proceed as above.

OPTIONAL TOPPING

Rich Egg Nog Cream: In large bowl, combine 1½ cups canned Borden® Egg Nog, chilled, and 1 (4-serving size) package *instant* vanilla flavor pudding mix; mix well. Whip 1 cup (½ pint) Borden® or Meadow Gold® Whipping Cream; fold into egg nog mixture. Chill. Use as topping for pie, cake or fruit. (Makes about 3½ cups)

IMPOSSIBLE PIE

Makes one 10-inch pie

 1 (14-ounce) can Eagle® Brand
     Sweetened Condensed Milk
     (NOT evaporated milk)
1½ cups water
 ½ cup biscuit baking mix
 3 eggs
 ¼ cup margarine or butter,
     softened
1½ teaspoons vanilla extract
 1 cup flaked coconut

Preheat oven to 350°. In blender container, combine all ingredients except coconut. Blend on low speed 3 minutes. Pour into greased *10-inch* pie plate; let stand 5 minutes. Sprinkle with coconut. Carefully place in oven; bake 35 to 40 minutes or until knife inserted near edge comes out clean. Cool slightly; serve warm or cooled. Refrigerate leftovers.

TIP: Pie can be baked in greased 9-inch pie plate but it will be extremely full.

★★★★
APPLE CHESS PIE

Makes one 9-inch pie

1 (9-inch) unbaked pastry shell
4 eggs
1 (14-ounce) can Eagle® Brand
    Sweetened Condensed Milk
    (NOT evaporated milk)
1 cup applesauce
½ cup margarine or butter, melted
½ cup shredded all-purpose apple
3 tablespoons ReaLemon® Lemon
    Juice from Concentrate
2 tablespoons cornmeal

Preheat oven to 425°. Bake pastry shell 8 minutes; remove from oven. Reduce oven temperature to 350°. Meanwhile, in large mixer bowl, beat eggs. Add remaining ingredients; mix well. Pour into prepared pastry shell. Bake 40 minutes or until knife inserted near center comes out clean. Cool. Serve warm or chilled. Garnish as desired. Refrigerate leftovers.

PINEAPPLE CHESS PIE: Omit applesauce, shredded apple and ReaLemon® brand. Reduce margarine or butter to ⅓ cup. Add 1 (8-ounce) can juice-pack crushed pineapple, *undrained,* and ½ cup pineapple juice. Proceed as above.

★★★★
PEACHY MINCE PIE WITH CHEDDAR CRUST

Makes one 9-inch pie

1 (9-ounce) package pie crust mix
1 cup (4 ounces) shredded sharp
  cheddar cheese
1 jar None Such® Ready-to-Use
  Mincemeat (Regular *or*
  Brandy & Rum)
1 (16-ounce) can peach slices,
  drained
1 egg yolk plus 2 tablespoons
  water, optional

Place rack in lowest position in oven; preheat oven to 425°. Prepare pie crust mix as package directs for 2-crust pie, adding cheese to dry mix. Turn mincemeat into pastry-lined 9-inch pie plate. Top with peach slices. Cover with top crust; seal and flute. Cut slits in top crust. For a more golden crust, mix egg yolk and water; brush over entire surface of pie. Bake 20 minutes or until golden. Serve warm or cooled.

★★★★
STREUSEL-TOPPED APPLE CUSTARD PIE

Makes one 9-inch pie

1 (9-inch) unbaked pastry shell
1½ pounds all-purpose apples, cored, pared and sliced (about 4 cups)
2 eggs
1 (14-ounce) can Eagle® Brand Sweetened Condensed Milk (NOT evaporated milk)
¼ cup margarine or butter, melted
½ teaspoon ground cinnamon
   Dash ground nutmeg
½ cup firmly packed light brown sugar
½ cup unsifted flour
¼ cup cold margarine or butter
¼ cup chopped nuts

Place rack in lowest position in oven; preheat oven to 425°. Arrange apples in pastry shell. In medium bowl, beat eggs. Add sweetened condensed milk, melted margarine, cinnamon and nutmeg; mix well. Pour over apples. In medium bowl, combine sugar and flour; cut in cold margarine until crumbly. Stir in nuts. Sprinkle over pie. Bake 10 minutes. Reduce oven temperature to 375°; bake 35 to 40 minutes longer or until golden brown. Cool. Refrigerate leftovers.

★★★★
COCONUT CUSTARD PIE

Makes one 9-inch pie

1 (9-inch) unbaked pastry shell
1 cup flaked coconut
3 eggs
1 (14-ounce) can Eagle® Brand
    Sweetened Condensed Milk
    (NOT evaporated milk)
1¼ cups water
  1 teaspoon vanilla extract
  ¼ teaspoon salt
  ⅛ teaspoon ground nutmeg

Preheat oven to 425°. Reserving *½ cup* coconut, toast remainder. Bake pastry shell 8 minutes; cool slightly. Meanwhile, in medium bowl, beat eggs. Add sweetened condensed milk, water, vanilla, salt and nutmeg; mix well. Stir in reserved *½ cup* coconut. Pour into prepared pastry shell. Sprinkle with toasted coconut. Bake 10 minutes. Reduce oven temperature to 350°; bake 25 to 30 minutes longer or until knife inserted near center comes out clean. Cool. Chill if desired. Garnish as desired. Refrigerate leftovers.

CUSTARD PIE: Omit coconut. Proceed as above.

★★★★
MINCE VELVET PIE

Makes one 9-inch pie

1 (9-inch) unbaked pastry shell
1 (14-ounce) can Eagle® Brand
    Sweetened Condensed Milk
    (NOT evaporated milk)
2 eggs
1⅓ cups (one-half jar) None Such®
    Ready-to-Use Mincemeat
    (Regular *or* Brandy & Rum)
⅓ cup ReaLime® Lime Juice from
    Concentrate
⅛ teaspoon salt
1 (8-ounce) container Borden® or
    Meadow Gold® Sour Cream,
    at room temperature
2 tablespoons sugar
½ teaspoon vanilla extract

Preheat oven to 375°. Bake pastry shell 15 minutes. Remove from oven; reduce oven temperature to 350°. Meanwhile, in large mixer bowl, beat sweetened condensed milk and eggs. Stir in mincemeat, ReaLime® brand and salt. Pour into prepared pastry shell; bake 20 minutes. Meanwhile, in small bowl, combine sour cream, sugar and vanilla; spread over pie. Bake 10 minutes longer. Cool. Chill 3 hours or until set. Garnish as desired. Refrigerate leftovers.

Mince Velvet Pie

Chocolate Amaretto Pie

★★★★
CHOCOLATE AMARETTO PIE

Makes one 9-inch pie

1 (9-inch) unbaked pastry shell
1 (3-ounce) package cream cheese,
    softened
2 (1-ounce) squares unsweetened
    chocolate, melted
⅛ teaspoon salt
1 (14-ounce) can Eagle® Brand
    Sweetened Condensed Milk
    (NOT evaporated milk)
2 eggs
¼ to ⅓ cup amaretto liqueur
1 cup sliced or chopped almonds,
    toasted if desired

Preheat oven to 350°. In large mixer bowl, beat cheese, chocolate and salt until well blended. Gradually beat in sweetened condensed milk until smooth. Add eggs; mix well. Stir in liqueur and almonds. Pour into pastry shell. Bake 30 to 35 minutes or until center is set. Cool. Serve warm or chilled. Garnish as desired. Refrigerate leftovers.

Apple Walnut Upside-Down Pie

★★★★
PUMPKIN
EGG NOG PIE

Makes one 9-inch pie

1 (9-inch) unbaked pastry shell
1 (16-ounce) can pumpkin
   (2 cups)
1½ cups Borden® or Meadow
   Gold® Egg Nog
2 eggs
½ cup sugar
½ teaspoon ground cinnamon
½ teaspoon salt
¼ teaspoon ground cloves
¼ teaspoon ground ginger

Preheat oven to 425°. In large mixer bowl, combine all ingredients except pastry shell; mix well. Pour into pastry shell. Bake 15 minutes. Reduce oven temperature to 350°; bake 40 to 45 minutes longer or until knife inserted near edge comes out clean. Cool. Refrigerate leftovers.

★★★★
APPLE WALNUT
UPSIDE-DOWN PIE

Makes one 9-inch pie

Pastry for 2-crust pie
¼ cup firmly packed light brown
   sugar
2 tablespoons margarine or
   butter, melted
½ cup chopped walnuts
2 pounds all-purpose apples,
   cored, pared and sliced (about
   5 cups)
⅔ to 1 cup granulated sugar
2 to 3 tablespoons flour
2 tablespoons ReaLemon® Lemon
   Juice from Concentrate
1 teaspoon ground cinnamon

Preheat oven to 400°. In 9-inch pie plate, combine brown sugar and margarine; spread over bottom. Sprinkle nuts evenly over sugar mixture. Divide pastry in half; roll each into 12-inch circle. Carefully line prepared pie plate with 1 pastry circle; *do not press* into nut mixture. Trim even with edge of plate. Combine remaining ingredients; turn into prepared pie plate. Cover with remaining pastry circle; prick with fork. Trim top crust even with edge of plate; seal crust edges with water. Roll edges *toward center* of pie (crust edge should *not* touch rim of plate). Place aluminum foil-lined baking sheet on bottom oven rack to catch drippings. Bake 40 to 45 minutes or until golden brown. Let stand 2 minutes; carefully run knife tip around edge of pie plate to loosen pie. Invert onto serving plate. Serve warm with ice cream if desired.

MINCE RASPBERRY COBBLER

Makes one 8-inch pie

Pastry for 1-crust pie
1 jar None Such® Ready-to-Use
   Mincemeat (Regular *or*
   Brandy & Rum)
1 (10-ounce) package frozen red
   raspberries in syrup, thawed
1 tablespoon cornstarch
1 egg yolk plus 2 tablespoons
   water

Preheat oven to 425°. In medium
bowl, combine mincemeat, raspberries
and cornstarch. Turn into 8-inch
square baking dish. Roll pastry to
9-inch square; cut slits near center.
Place pastry over filling; turn under
edges, seal and flute. Mix egg yolk and
water; brush over entire surface of pie.
Bake 30 minutes or until golden
brown. Serve warm with ice cream
if desired.

CRANBERRY MINCE STREUSEL PIE

Makes one 9-inch pie

1 (9-inch) unbaked pastry shell
1 cup unsifted flour
½ cup sugar
¼ teaspoon baking soda
¼ teaspoon salt
3 tablespoons vegetable oil
2 tablespoons Borden® or
   Meadow Gold® Milk
¼ cup chopped nuts
1 (14-ounce) container cranberry-
   orange sauce
1 jar None Such® Ready-to-Use
   Mincemeat (Regular *or*
   Brandy & Rum)

Place rack in lowest position in oven;
preheat oven to 425°. In small bowl,
mix flour, sugar, baking soda and
salt. Stir in oil, milk and nuts until
crumbly. Spread cranberry-orange
sauce on bottom of pastry shell.
Sprinkle with half the crumb mixture.
Spread mincemeat on top; sprinkle
with remaining crumb mixture. Bake
15 minutes. Reduce oven temperature
to 350°; bake 40 minutes longer or
until bubbly. Serve warm or cooled.
Garnish as desired.

Cranberry Mince Streusel Pie

★★★★
UNBELIEVABLE LEMON COCONUT PIE

Makes one 10-inch pie

- 1 (14-ounce) can Eagle® Brand Sweetened Condensed Milk (NOT evaporated milk)
- 1 cup water
- ½ cup ReaLemon® Lemon Juice from Concentrate
- ½ cup biscuit baking mix
- 3 eggs
- ¼ cup margarine or butter, softened
- 1½ teaspoons vanilla extract
- 1 (3½-ounce) can flaked coconut (1⅓ cups)

Preheat oven to 350°. In blender container, combine all ingredients except coconut. Blend on low speed 3 minutes. Pour into greased *10-inch* pie plate; let stand 5 minutes. Sprinkle with coconut. Bake 35 to 40 minutes or until knife inserted near edge comes out clean. Cool slightly; serve warm or cooled. Refrigerate leftovers.

Create-a-Crust Apple Custard Pie

★★★★
CREATE-A-CRUST APPLE CUSTARD PIE

Makes one 10-inch pie

- 2 medium all-purpose apples, cored, pared and sliced
- 1 tablespoon ReaLemon® Lemon Juice from Concentrate
- ½ cup plus 2 tablespoons biscuit baking mix
- 1 (14-ounce) can Eagle® Brand Sweetened Condensed Milk (NOT evaporated milk)
- 1½ cups water
- 3 eggs
- ¼ cup margarine or butter, softened
- 1½ teaspoons vanilla extract
- ½ teaspoon ground cinnamon
- ½ teaspoon ground nutmeg Crumb Topping

Preheat oven to 350°. Toss apples with ReaLemon® brand then *2 tablespoons* biscuit mix; arrange in buttered 10-inch pie plate. In blender, combine remaining ingredients except Crumb Topping. Blend on low speed 3 minutes; let stand 5 minutes. Pour over apples; top with Crumb Topping. Bake 35 minutes or until golden. Cool. Garnish as desired. Refrigerate leftovers.

CRUMB TOPPING: In small bowl, combine ½ cup *each* biscuit baking mix and firmly packed brown sugar; cut in ¼ cup cold margarine or butter until crumbly. Add ¼ cup chopped nuts. (Makes about 2 cups)

Fudgy Pecan Pie

FUDGY PECAN PIE

Makes one 9-inch pie

1 (9-inch) unbaked pastry shell
1 (4-ounce) package sweet cooking
  chocolate, *or* 2 (1-ounce)
  squares unsweetened
  chocolate
¼ cup margarine or butter
1 (14-ounce) can Eagle® Brand
  Sweetened Condensed Milk
  (NOT evaporated milk)
½ cup water
2 eggs, beaten
1 teaspoon vanilla extract
⅛ teaspoon salt
1¼ cups pecan halves or pieces

Preheat oven to 350°. In medium
saucepan, over low heat, melt
chocolate with margarine. Stir in
sweetened condensed milk, water and
eggs; *mix well*. Remove from heat; stir
in remaining ingredients except pastry
shell. Pour into pastry shell. Bake 40
to 45 minutes or until center is set.
Cool slightly. Serve warm or chilled.
Garnish as desired. Refrigerate
leftovers.

TRADITIONAL MINCE PIE

Makes one 9-inch pie

Pastry for 2-crust pie
1 jar None Such® Ready-to-Use
  Mincemeat (Regular *or*
  Brandy & Rum)
1 egg yolk plus 2 tablespoons
  water, optional

Place rack in lowest position in oven;
preheat oven to 425°. Turn mincemeat
into pastry-lined 9-inch pie plate.
Cover with top crust; cut slits near
center. Seal and flute. For a more
golden crust, mix egg yolk and water;
brush over entire surface of pie. Bake
30 minutes or until golden. Cool
slightly. Garnish as desired.

TIP: Prepare pastry for 9- or 10-inch
2-crust pie. In saucepan, combine 2
(9- ounce) packages None Such®
Condensed Mincemeat, crumbled,
and 3 cups water; bring to a boil.
Cook and stir 1 minute. Cool. Turn
into pastry-lined pie plate. Proceed as
above.

Almond Pumpkin Pie

MINCEMEAT TURNOVERS

Makes 8 turnovers

1 (9-ounce) package None Such® Condensed Mincemeat, crumbled
¾ cup orange juice
½ cup chopped nuts
1 teaspoon grated orange rind
2 (3-ounce) packages cream cheese, cut into pieces
1 (11-ounce) package pie crust mix
1 egg yolk plus 2 tablespoons water

Preheat oven to 375°. In small saucepan, combine mincemeat and orange juice. Over medium heat, bring mixture to a boil; cook and stir 1 minute. Remove from heat; stir in nuts and rind. In large bowl, cut cheese into pie crust mix until crumbly; form into 2 balls. On floured surface, roll each ball of dough into a 12-inch square; cut into 4 (6-inch) squares. Place scant ¼ cup mincemeat mixture just off center on each pastry square. Fold pastry in half diagonally over filling; seal by pressing edges together with fork. Place on ungreased baking sheet; cut slit near center of each turnover. Mix egg yolk and water; brush over entire surface of pastry. Bake 25 minutes or until golden brown. Serve warm.

★ ★ ★ ★

ALMOND PUMPKIN PIE

Makes one 9-inch pie

1 (9-inch) unbaked pastry shell
1 (16-ounce) can pumpkin (2 cups)
1 (14-ounce) can Eagle® Brand Sweetened Condensed Milk (NOT evaporated milk)
2 eggs
1 teaspoon almond extract
½ teaspoon ground cinnamon
1 (6-ounce) package almond brickle chips, *or* 1 cup almonds, toasted and finely chopped

Preheat oven to 425°. In large mixer bowl, combine all ingredients except pastry shell and brickle chips; mix well. Stir in ½ *cup* brickle chips. Pour into pastry shell. Top with remaining brickle chips. Bake 15 minutes. Reduce oven temperature to 350°; bake 30 minutes longer or until knife inserted near center comes out clean. Cool. Refrigerate leftovers.

★ ★ ★ ★
APPLE STREUSEL MINCE PIE

Makes one 9-inch pie

1 (9-inch) unbaked pastry shell
1 pound all-purpose apples,
    cored, pared and thinly sliced
    (about 3 cups)
½ cup plus 3 tablespoons unsifted
    flour
2 tablespoons margarine or
    butter, melted
1 jar None Such® Ready-to-Use
    Mincemeat (Regular *or*
    Brandy & Rum)
¼ cup firmly packed light brown
    sugar
1 teaspoon ground cinnamon
⅓ cup cold margarine or butter
¼ cup chopped nuts

Place rack in lowest position in oven; preheat oven to 425°. In large bowl, toss apples with *3 tablespoons* flour and melted margarine; arrange in pastry shell. Top with mincemeat. In medium bowl, combine remaining *½ cup* flour, sugar and cinnamon; cut in cold margarine until crumbly. Add nuts; sprinkle over mincemeat. Bake 10 minutes. Reduce oven temperature to 375°; bake 25 minutes longer or until golden. Cool.

TIP: 1 (9-ounce) package None Such® Condensed Mincemeat, reconstituted as package directs, can be substituted for None Such® Ready-to-Use Mincemeat.

OZEN ⋆ PIES

When the occasion calls for a special dessert, create a fabulous frozen pie. These make-ahead pies are the perfect finale for a holiday feast or patio party. Try Lemon Custard Ice Cream Pie or Frozen Chocolate Mousse Pie for a real celebration!

Pictured here is Frozen Peanut Butter Pie; see page 54 for recipe.

★★★★
FROZEN PEANUT BUTTER PIE

Makes one 9- or 10-inch pie

Chocolate Crunch Crust
1 (8-ounce) package cream cheese, softened
1 (14-ounce) can Eagle® Brand Sweetened Condensed Milk (NOT evaporated milk)
¾ cup peanut butter
2 tablespoons ReaLemon® Lemon Juice from Concentrate
1 teaspoon vanilla extract
1 cup (½ pint) Borden® or Meadow Gold® Whipping Cream, whipped, *or* 1 (4-ounce) container frozen non-dairy whipped topping, thawed (1¾ cups)
Chocolate fudge ice cream topping

Prepare Chocolate Crunch Crust. In large mixer bowl, beat cheese until fluffy; gradually beat in sweetened condensed milk then peanut butter until smooth. Stir in ReaLemon® brand and vanilla. Fold in whipped cream. Turn into prepared crust. Drizzle topping over pie. Freeze 4 hours or until firm. Freeze leftovers.

CHOCOLATE CRUNCH CRUST:
In heavy saucepan, over low heat, melt ⅓ cup margarine or butter and 1 (6-ounce) package semi-sweet chocolate chips (1 cup). Remove from heat; gently stir in 2½ cups oven-toasted rice cereal until completely coated. Press on bottom and up side to rim of buttered 9- or 10-inch pie plate. Chill 30 minutes.

★★★★
MINCE ICE CREAM PIE IN COOKIE CRUST

Makes one 9-inch pie

¾ cup unsifted flour
½ cup quick-cooking oats
½ cup finely chopped nuts
¼ cup firmly packed brown sugar
⅓ cup margarine or butter, melted
1 (9-ounce) package None Such® Condensed Mincemeat, crumbled
¾ cup water
1 quart Borden® or Meadow Gold® Vanilla Ice Cream, slightly softened

Preheat oven to 400°. In medium bowl, combine flour, oats, nuts and sugar; add margarine. Mix well. Press firmly on bottom and up side to rim of 9-inch pie plate. Bake 15 minutes or until lightly browned. Cool. Meanwhile, in small saucepan, combine mincemeat and water. Bring to a boil; cook and stir 1 minute. Cool. Chill. Spoon half the ice cream into prepared crust. Top with 1 cup mincemeat, remaining ice cream then remaining mincemeat. Cover; freeze at least 2 hours. Remove from freezer 5 minutes before serving. Freeze leftovers.

★ ★ ★ ★

FROZEN STRAWBERRY MARGARITA PIE

Makes one 9-inch pie

1¼ cups *finely* crushed Seyfert's®
    Pretzels
¼ cup sugar
½ cup plus 2 tablespoons
    margarine or butter, melted
1 (14-ounce) can Eagle® Brand
    Sweetened Condensed Milk
    (NOT evaporated milk)
1 cup chopped fresh or thawed
    frozen unsweetened
    strawberries
¼ cup ReaLime® Lime Juice from
    Concentrate
3 to 4 tablespoons tequila
2 tablespoons triple sec or other
    orange-flavored liqueur
    Red food coloring, optional
1 cup (½ pint) Borden® or
    Meadow Gold® Whipping
    Cream, whipped

Combine pretzel crumbs, sugar and margarine; press firmly on bottom and up side to rim of lightly buttered 9-inch pie plate. In large bowl, combine sweetened condensed milk, chopped strawberries, ReaLime® brand, tequila, triple sec and food coloring if desired; mix well. Fold in whipped cream. Pour into prepared crust. Freeze 4 hours or until firm. Let stand 10 minutes before serving. Garnish as desired. Freeze leftovers.

FROZEN MARGARITA PIE:
Omit strawberries and red food coloring. Increase ReaLime® brand to ⅓ cup and add green food coloring if desired. Proceed as above. Freeze 4 hours. Garnish as desired. Freeze leftovers.

Left to right: Frozen Margarita Pie, Frozen Strawberry Margarita Pie

Frozen Peach Cream Pies

In large mixer bowl, beat cheese until fluffy. Gradually beat in sweetened condensed milk then pureed peaches, ReaLemon® brand, extract and food coloring if desired. Fold in whipped topping. Pour equal portions into crusts. Freeze 4 hours or until firm. Remove from freezer 5 minutes before serving. Garnish with peach slices. Freeze leftovers.

=★★★★=

FROZEN PEACH CREAM PIES

Makes 2 pies

1 (8-ounce) package cream cheese, softened
1 (14-ounce) can Eagle® Brand Sweetened Condensed Milk (NOT evaporated milk)
1½ cups pureed fresh or thawed frozen peaches
1 tablespoon ReaLemon® Lemon Juice from Concentrate
¼ teaspoon almond extract
Yellow and red food coloring, optional
1 (8-ounce) container frozen non-dairy whipped topping, thawed (3½ cups)
2 (6-ounce) packaged graham cracker crumb pie crusts
Peach slices

=★★★★=

MAI TAI PIE

Makes one 9-inch pie

Coconut Crust
1 (8-ounce) package cream cheese, softened
1 (14-ounce) can Eagle® Brand Sweetened Condensed Milk (NOT evaporated milk)
1 (6-ounce) can frozen orange juice concentrate, thawed
3 tablespoons light rum
1 tablespoon orange-flavored liqueur
1 cup (½ pint) Borden® or Meadow Gold® Whipping Cream, stiffly whipped

Prepare Coconut Crust. In large mixer bowl, beat cheese until fluffy. Gradually beat in sweetened condensed milk then juice concentrate until smooth. Stir in rum and liqueur. Fold in whipped cream. Pour into prepared crust. Freeze or chill 4 hours or until set. Freeze or refrigerate leftovers.

COCONUT CRUST: Combine 1 (7-ounce) package flaked coconut (2⅔ cups), toasted, with ⅓ cup margarine or butter, melted; mix well. Press firmly on bottom and up side to rim of 9-inch pie plate. Chill.

★★★★
MUD PIE

Makes one 9-inch pie

1 (14-ounce) can Eagle® Brand
    Sweetened Condensed Milk
    (NOT evaporated milk)
4 teaspoons vanilla extract
2 cups (1 pint) Borden® or
    Meadow Gold® Whipping
    Cream, whipped *(do not use
    non-dairy whipped topping)*
1 cup coarsely crushed creme-
    filled chocolate sandwich
    cookies (about 10 cookies)
1 (9-inch) chocolate crumb crust
    Chocolate fudge ice cream
        topping or chocolate-flavored
        syrup
    Chopped nuts

In large bowl, combine sweetened
condensed milk and vanilla. Fold in
whipped cream then cookies. Pour into
9×5-inch loaf pan or other 2-quart
container; cover. Freeze 6 hours or
until firm. Scoop ice cream into
prepared crust. Drizzle with topping.
Garnish with nuts. Freeze leftovers.

FROZEN CHOCOLATE MOUSSE PIE

Makes one 9-inch pie

2 cups finely crushed creme-filled
  chocolate sandwich cookies
  (about 20 cookies)
¼ cup margarine or butter, melted
1 (6-ounce) package semi-sweet
  chocolate chips (1 cup), *or*
  4 (1-ounce) squares semi-
  sweet chocolate, melted
1 (14-ounce) can Eagle® Brand
  Sweetened Condensed Milk
  (NOT evaporated milk)
1½ teaspoons vanilla extract
1 cup (½ pint) Borden® or
  Meadow Gold® Whipping
  Cream, stiffly whipped

Combine crumbs and margarine; press
on bottom and up side to rim of
lightly buttered 9-inch pie plate. Chill.
In large mixer bowl, beat chocolate
with sweetened condensed milk and
vanilla until well blended. Chill 10 to
15 minutes. Fold in whipped cream.
Pour into prepared crust. Freeze
6 hours or until firm. Garnish as
desired. Freeze leftovers.

Frozen Chocolate Mousse Pie

HAWAIIAN ICE CREAM PIE

Makes one 9-inch pie

2 egg whites
¼ teaspoon cream of tartar
2 tablespoons sugar
1 (7-ounce) package flaked
  coconut (2⅔ cups)
1 quart Borden® or Meadow
  Gold® Vanilla Ice Cream
1 quart Borden® or Meadow
  Gold® Orange Sherbet
  Pineapple Sauce
  Macadamia nuts, chopped and
  toasted, optional

Preheat oven to 350°. In small mixer
bowl, beat egg whites and cream of
tartar to soft peaks. Gradually add
sugar, beating until stiff but not dry.
Fold in coconut. Spread on bottom
and up side of *well-buttered* 9-inch
pie plate to form crust. Bake 15 to
20 minutes or until coconut *begins*
to brown. Cool to room temperature.
Scoop ice cream and sherbet into
crust. Just before serving, top with
Pineapple Sauce and nuts if desired.
Freeze leftovers.

PINEAPPLE SAUCE: In medium
saucepan, combine 1 tablespoon
each sugar and water, 1 teaspoon
each cornstarch and ReaLemon®
Lemon Juice from Concentrate and
1 (8-ounce) can juice-pack crushed
pineapple. Over medium heat, cook
and stir until slightly thickened and
clear. Stir in 1 tablespoon margarine
or butter until melted. Cool. (Makes
about 1 cup)

★ ★ ★ ★

FROZEN ORANGE CLOUD PIE

Makes one 9-inch pie

2 cups vanilla wafer crumbs
  (about 48 wafers)
⅓ cup margarine or butter, melted
1 (14-ounce) can Eagle® Brand
  Sweetened Condensed Milk
  (NOT evaporated milk)
½ cup orange carbonated beverage
2 to 3 teaspoons grated orange
  rind
  Red and yellow food coloring,
  optional
2 cups (1 pint) Borden ® or
  Meadow Gold® Whipping
  Cream, stiffly whipped

Combine crumbs and margarine; press firmly on bottom and up side to rim of 9-inch pie plate. In large bowl, combine sweetened condensed milk, carbonated beverage, rind and food coloring if desired; mix well. Fold in whipped cream. Pour into prepared crust. Freeze 6 hours or until firm. Let stand 10 minutes before serving. Garnish as desired. Freeze leftovers.

★ ★ ★ ★

MINCE ICE CREAM ANGEL PIE

Makes one 9-inch pie

  3 egg whites
½ teaspoon vanilla extract
¼ teaspoon cream of tartar
½ cup sugar
  1 quart Borden® or Meadow
      Gold® Vanilla or Coffee Ice
      Cream, slightly softened
  1 quart Borden® or Meadow
      Gold® Orange Sherbet,
      slightly softened
1⅓ cups (one-half jar) None Such®
      Ready-to-Use Mincemeat
      (Regular *or* Brandy & Rum)
  1 tablespoon orange-flavored
      liqueur
½ teaspoon grated orange rind

Preheat oven to 275°. In small mixer bowl, beat egg whites, vanilla and cream of tartar to soft peaks. Gradually add sugar, beating until stiff but not dry. Spread on bottom and up side of *well-buttered* 9-inch pie plate to form crust. Bake 1 hour. Turn oven off; leave crust in oven 1 hour. Cool to room temperature. Scoop ice cream and sherbet into prepared crust, alternating flavors; freeze. In small saucepan, combine mincemeat, liqueur and rind. Heat through, stirring occasionally. Spoon sauce over pie. Freeze leftovers.

★★★★

FROZEN FLUFFY STRAWBERRY PIE

Makes one 9-inch pie

2½ cups flaked coconut, toasted
⅓ cup margarine or butter, melted
1 (3-ounce) package cream cheese, softened
1 (14-ounce) can Eagle® Brand Sweetened Condensed Milk (NOT evaporated milk)
2½ cups fresh or thawed frozen unsweetened strawberries, mashed or pureed (about 1½ cups)
3 tablespoons ReaLemon® Lemon Juice from Concentrate
1 cup (½ pint) Borden® or Meadow Gold® Whipping Cream, whipped
Additional fresh strawberries, optional

Combine coconut and margarine; press firmly on bottom and up side to rim of 9-inch pie plate. In large mixer bowl, beat cheese until fluffy; gradually beat in sweetened condensed milk until smooth. Stir in pureed strawberries and ReaLemon® brand. Fold in whipped cream. Pour into prepared crust (mixture should mound slightly). Freeze 4 hours or until firm. Before serving, garnish with fresh strawberries if desired. Freeze leftovers.

TIP: 1 (9-inch) baked pastry shell can be substituted for coconut crust.

Lemon Custard Ice Cream Pie

Preheat oven to 275°. In small mixer bowl, beat *3 egg whites* (reserve yolks), vanilla and cream of tartar to soft peaks. Gradually add *½ cup* sugar, beating until stiff but not dry. Spread on bottom and up side to rim of *well-buttered* 9-inch pie plate to form crust. Bake 1 hour. Turn oven off; leave crust in oven 1 hour. Cool to room temperature. Meanwhile, in medium saucepan, melt margarine. Add remaining *1 cup* sugar, ReaLemon® brand and salt; mix well. In small bowl, beat remaining *2 eggs* and reserved *3 egg yolks;* gradually add to lemon mixture. Over low heat, cook and stir constantly until thickened. Cool to room temperature. Spoon one-third of the sauce into crust then half the ice cream. Repeat layering, ending with sauce. Freeze 6 hours or until firm. Freeze leftovers.

====★★★★====

LEMON CUSTARD ICE CREAM PIE

Makes one 9-inch pie

   5 eggs
½ teaspoon vanilla extract
¼ teaspoon cream of tartar
1½ cups sugar
½ cup margarine or butter
½ cup ReaLemon® Lemon Juice
   from Concentrate
¼ teaspoon salt
   1 quart Borden® or Meadow
   Gold® Vanilla Ice Cream,
   slightly softened

====★★★★====

FRUIT & ICE CREAM PIZZA

Makes one 12-inch pizza

½ (20-ounce) package refrigerated
   cookie dough, any flavor
1 quart Borden® or Meadow
   Gold® Vanilla Ice Cream,
   softened
   Assorted cut-up fresh or canned
   fruits
½ cup pineapple or strawberry ice
   cream topping

Preheat oven to 350°. Press cookie dough into greased 12-inch pizza pan or into 12-inch circle on greased baking sheet; bake 12 to 14 minutes. Cool. Spoon ice cream onto crust; freeze until firm. Top with fruit and drizzle with topping. Freeze leftovers.

★ ★ ★ ★

FROZEN CRANBERRY CHEESE PIE

Makes one 9-inch pie

1½ cups vanilla wafer crumbs
    (about 36 wafers)
  6 tablespoons margarine or
    butter, melted
  2 (3-ounce) packages cream
    cheese, softened
  1 (14-ounce) can Eagle® Brand
    Sweetened Condensed Milk
    (NOT evaporated milk)
⅓ cup ReaLemon® Lemon Juice
    from Concentrate
  1 teaspoon vanilla extract
    Red food coloring, optional
  1 (16-ounce) can whole berry
    cranberry sauce
    Whipped cream

Combine crumbs and margarine; press firmly on bottom and up side to rim of 9-inch pie plate. Chill. Meanwhile, in large mixer bowl, beat cheese until fluffy. Gradually beat in sweetened condensed milk until smooth. Stir in ReaLemon® brand, vanilla and food coloring if desired. Reserving ½ *cup* cranberry sauce, add remainder to cheese mixture. Pour into prepared crust. Cover; freeze 6 hours or until firm. Just before serving, garnish with whipped cream and reserved cranberry sauce. Freeze leftovers.

Frozen Cranberry Cheese Pie

★ ★ ★ ★

CHOCO-NUTTY SUNDAE PIE

Makes one 9-inch pie

  1 cup chocolate-flavored syrup
1¼ cups vanilla wafer crumbs
    (about 30 wafers)
  1 (3½-ounce) can flaked coconut
    (1⅓ cups)
  1 cup chopped nuts
  1 teaspoon vanilla extract
2½ quarts Borden® or Meadow
    Gold® Ice Cream, any flavor,
    slightly softened
    Additional chocolate-flavored
    syrup

In large bowl, combine ½ *cup* syrup, crumbs, coconut, nuts and vanilla; mix well. With buttered hands, press mixture on bottom and up side to rim of well-buttered 9-inch pie plate. Spoon ½ *quart* ice cream into crust; top with remaining ½ *cup* syrup. Top with scoops of remaining ice cream. Drizzle with additional syrup. Freeze 6 hours or until firm. Freeze leftovers.

★★★★

elight dessert lovers
with their favorite
flavor chilled pies.
There's refreshing
ReaLemon Meringue,
Key Lime, Banana
Cream and Fudge
Deluxe pies. And what
could be more
memorable than
scrumptious Cherry
Cheese Pie?

★★★★

Pictured here is Cherry Cheese Pie;
see page 66 for recipe.

★★★★
CHERRY CHEESE PIE

Makes one 9-inch pie

1 (9-inch) graham cracker crumb
    crust or baked pastry shell
1 (8-ounce) package cream cheese,
    softened
1 (14-ounce) can Eagle® Brand
    Sweetened Condensed Milk
    (NOT evaporated milk)
⅓ cup ReaLemon® Lemon Juice
    from Concentrate
1 teaspoon vanilla extract
1 (21-ounce) can cherry pie
    filling, chilled

In large mixer bowl, beat cheese until
fluffy. Gradually beat in sweetened
condensed milk until smooth. Stir in
ReaLemon® brand and vanilla. Pour
into prepared crust. Chill 3 hours or
until set. Top with desired amount of
pie filling before serving. Refrigerate
leftovers.

TOPPING VARIATIONS

Ambrosia: Omit cherry pie filling. In
small saucepan, combine ½ cup
Bama® Peach *or* Apricot Preserves,
¼ cup flaked coconut, 2 tablespoons
orange juice *or* orange-flavored
liqueur and 2 teaspoons cornstarch;
cook and stir until thickened. Remove
from heat. Arrange fresh orange
sections over top of pie; top with
coconut mixture. Chill.

Blueberry: Omit cherry pie filling. In
medium saucepan, combine ¼ cup
sugar and 1 tablespoon cornstarch; mix
well. Add ½ cup water, 2 tablespoons
ReaLemon® brand then 2 cups fresh or
dry-pack frozen blueberries; mix well.
Bring to a boil; reduce heat and
simmer 3 minutes or until thickened
and clear. Cool 10 minutes. Spread
over pie. Chill.

★★★★
FRESH STRAWBERRY PIE

Makes one 9-inch pie

1 (9-inch) baked pastry shell
1¼ cups sugar
1 tablespoon cornstarch
1½ cups water
3 tablespoons ReaLemon® Lemon
    Juice from Concentrate
1 (4-serving size) package
    strawberry flavor gelatin
1 quart fresh strawberries,
    cleaned and hulled (about
    1½ pounds)

In medium saucepan, combine
sugar and cornstarch; add water and
ReaLemon® brand. Over high heat,
bring to a boil. Reduce heat; cook,
stirring occasionally, until slightly
thickened and clear, 4 to 5 minutes.
Add gelatin; stir until dissolved. Chill
until thickened but not set, about 1
hour. Stir in strawberries; spoon into
prepared pastry shell. Chill 4 to
6 hours or until set. Refrigerate
leftovers.

MICROWAVE: In 2-quart glass
measure, combine sugar and
cornstarch; add water and ReaLemon®
brand. Cook on 100% power (high)
6 to 8 minutes, or until slightly
thickened and bubbly, stirring every
2 minutes. Proceed as above.

★★★★
FUDGE DELUXE PIE

Makes one 9-inch pie

1 (9-inch) baked pastry shell
3 (1-ounce) squares unsweetened
    or semi-sweet chocolate
1 (14-ounce) can Eagle® Brand
    Sweetened Condensed Milk
    (NOT evaporated milk)
¼ teaspoon salt
¼ cup water
2 egg yolks
1 teaspoon vanilla extract
1 cup (½ pint) Borden® or
    Meadow Gold® Whipping
    Cream
Additional whipped cream

In heavy saucepan, over medium heat, melt chocolate with sweetened condensed milk and salt. Cook and stir rapidly until *very thick* and bubbly, 5 to 8 minutes. Add water and egg yolks; cook and stir rapidly until mixture thickens and bubbles again. Remove from heat; stir in vanilla. Cool 15 minutes. *Chill thoroughly,* about 30 minutes; stir. In large mixer bowl, beat *1 cup* whipping cream until stiff; fold into cooled chocolate mixture. Pour into prepared pastry shell. Chill 3 hours or until set. Spread top with additional whipped cream; garnish as desired. Refrigerate leftovers.

Fluffy Grasshopper Pie

═══★★★★═══

FLUFFY GRASSHOPPER PIE

Makes one 9-inch pie

2 cups finely crushed creme-filled chocolate sandwich cookies (about 20 cookies)
¼ cup margarine or butter, melted
1 (8-ounce) package cream cheese, softened
1 (14-ounce) can Eagle® Brand Sweetened Condensed Milk (NOT evaporated milk)
3 tablespoons ReaLemon® Lemon Juice from Concentrate
¼ cup green creme de menthe
¼ cup white creme de cacao
1 (4-ounce) container frozen non-dairy whipped topping, thawed (1¾ cups)

Combine crumbs and margarine; press firmly on bottom and up side to rim of buttered 9-inch pie plate. Chill. Meanwhile, in large mixer bowl, beat cheese until fluffy. Gradually beat in sweetened condensed milk until smooth. Stir in ReaLemon® brand and liqueurs. Fold in whipped topping. Chill 20 minutes; pour into crust. Chill or freeze 4 hours or until set. Garnish as desired. Refrigerate or freeze leftovers.

═══★★★★═══

HAWAIIAN CHEESE PIE

Makes one 9-inch pie

1 (7-ounce) package flaked coconut (2⅔ cups), lightly toasted
⅓ cup margarine or butter, melted
1 (8-ounce) package cream cheese, softened
1 (14-ounce) can Eagle® Brand Sweetened Condensed Milk (NOT evaporated milk)
⅓ cup frozen orange juice concentrate, thawed
1 (8-ounce) can crushed pineapple, *well drained*
1½ teaspoons grated orange rind
Yellow food coloring, optional
1 (8-ounce) container frozen non-dairy whipped topping, thawed (3½ cups)

Preheat oven to 400°. Combine coconut and margarine; press on bottom and up side to rim of 9-inch pie plate. Bake 4 to 5 minutes or until *lightly browned*. Cool. In large mixer bowl, beat cheese until fluffy. Gradually beat in sweetened condensed milk until smooth then juice concentrate. Stir in pineapple, rind and food coloring if desired. Fold in whipped topping. Pour into prepared crust. Chill 3 hours or until set. Garnish as desired. Refrigerate leftovers.

====★★★★====

PINK LEMONADE PIE

Makes one 9-inch pie

1 (9-inch) baked pastry shell
1 (8-ounce) package cream cheese, softened
1 (14-ounce) can Eagle® Brand Sweetened Condensed Milk (NOT evaporated milk)
1 (6-ounce) can frozen pink lemonade concentrate, thawed
Red food coloring, optional
1 (4-ounce) container frozen non-dairy whipped topping, thawed (1¾ cups)
½ cup pink tinted coconut*

In large mixer bowl, beat cheese until fluffy. Gradually beat in sweetened condensed milk until smooth. Stir in lemonade concentrate and food coloring if desired. Fold in whipped topping. Pour into prepared pastry shell. Chill 4 hours or until set. Garnish with coconut. Refrigerate leftovers.

*TO TINT COCONUT: In small plastic bag or bowl, combine ½ cup flaked coconut, ½ teaspoon water and 2 drops red food coloring; shake or mix well.

Pink Lemonade Pie

Mini Fruit Cheese Tarts

====★★★★====

MINI FRUIT CHEESE TARTS

Makes 24 tarts

24 (2- or 3-inch) prepared tart-size crusts
1 (8-ounce) package cream cheese, softened
1 (14-ounce) can Eagle® Brand Sweetened Condensed Milk (NOT evaporated milk)
⅓ cup ReaLemon® Lemon Juice from Concentrate
1 teaspoon vanilla extract
Assorted fruit (strawberries, blueberries, bananas, raspberries, orange segments, cherries, kiwifruit, grapes or pineapple)
¼ cup Bama® Apple Jelly, melted

In large mixer bowl, beat cheese until fluffy. Gradually beat in sweetened condensed milk until smooth. Stir in ReaLemon® brand and vanilla. Spoon equal portions into crusts. Top with fruit; brush with jelly. Chill 2 hours or until set. Refrigerate leftovers.

★★★★

LEMON ANGEL PIE

Makes one 9-inch pie

Meringue Crust
1 (14-ounce) can Eagle® Brand
  Sweetened Condensed Milk
  (NOT evaporated milk)
⅓ cup ReaLemon® Lemon Juice
  from Concentrate
2 teaspoons grated lemon rind
  Yellow food coloring, optional
3 egg whites*
¼ teaspoon cream of tartar
1 cup (½ pint) Borden® or
  Meadow Gold® Whipping
  Cream, whipped

Prepare Meringue Crust. In large
bowl, combine sweetened condensed
milk, ReaLemon® brand, rind and
food coloring if desired; mix well. In
small mixer bowl, beat egg whites with
cream of tartar until stiff but not dry;
gently fold into sweetened condensed
milk mixture. Fold in whipped cream.
Pour into prepared crust. Chill 3 hours
or until set. Garnish as desired.
Refrigerate leftovers.

MERINGUE CRUST: Preheat oven
to 275°. In small mixer bowl, beat
3 egg whites, ½ teaspoon vanilla
extract and ¼ teaspoon cream of tartar
to soft peaks. Gradually add ½ cup
sugar, beating until stiff but not dry.
Spread on bottom and up side of *well-
buttered* 9-inch pie plate to form crust.
Bake 1 hour. Turn oven off; leave crust
in oven 1 hour. Cool to room
temperature.

*Use only Grade A clean, uncracked
eggs.

★ ★ ★ ★
FLUFFY YOGURT FRUIT PIE

Makes one 9-inch pie

1 (9-inch) graham cracker crumb
    crust or baked pastry shell
1 (8-ounce) package cream cheese,
    softened
1 (14-ounce) can Eagle® Brand
    Sweetened Condensed Milk
    (NOT evaporated milk)
1 (8-ounce) container Borden®
    Lite-Line® or Viva®
    Strawberry or other fruit
    Yogurt
2 tablespoons ReaLemon® Lemon
    Juice from Concentrate
  Red or other food coloring,
    optional
1 (8-ounce) container frozen non-
    dairy whipped topping,
    thawed (3½ cups)
  Strawberries or other fresh fruit
    and mint leaves

In large mixer bowl, beat cheese until fluffy. Gradually beat in sweetened condensed milk until smooth. Stir in yogurt, ReaLemon® brand and food coloring if desired. Fold in whipped topping. Pour into prepared crust. Chill 4 hours or until set. Garnish with strawberries. Refrigerate leftovers.

Spirited Chocolate Cream Tarts

SPIRITED CHOCOLATE CREAM TARTS

Makes 10 to 12 tarts

10 to 12 (3-inch) prepared tart-size
   crusts
1 (14-ounce) can Eagle® Brand
   Sweetened Condensed Milk
   (NOT evaporated milk)
2 tablespoons orange-, almond-
   or coffee-flavored liqueur
   or brandy
2 tablespoons cold water
1 (4-serving size) package *instant*
   chocolate flavor pudding mix
¼ cup unsweetened cocoa
1 cup (½ pint) Borden® or
   Meadow Gold® Whipping
   Cream, whipped

In large mixer bowl, beat sweetened
condensed milk, liqueur and water
until well blended; add pudding mix
and cocoa. Beat until smooth. Chill
5 minutes. Fold in whipped cream.
Spoon equal portions into crusts.
Chill. Garnish as desired. Refrigerate
leftovers.

BANANA MANDARIN CHEESE PIE

Makes one 9-inch pie

1 (9-inch) graham cracker crumb
   crust
1 (8-ounce) package cream cheese,
   softened
1 (14-ounce) can Eagle® Brand
   Sweetened Condensed Milk
   (NOT evaporated milk)
⅓ cup ReaLemon® Lemon Juice
   from Concentrate
1 teaspoon vanilla extract
3 medium bananas
   Additional ReaLemon® brand
1 (11-ounce) can mandarin orange
   segments, well drained

In large mixer bowl, beat cheese until
fluffy. Gradually beat in sweetened
condensed milk until smooth. Stir in
⅓ cup ReaLemon® brand and vanilla.
Slice *2 bananas;* dip in ReaLemon®
brand and drain. Line crust with
bananas and about *two-thirds* of the
orange segments. Pour filling over
fruit. Chill 3 hours or until set. Before
serving, slice remaining banana; dip in
ReaLemon® brand and drain. Garnish
top with banana slices and remaining
orange segments. Refrigerate leftovers.

Banana Mandarin Cheese Pie

KEY LIME PIE

Makes one 9- or 10-inch pie

1 (9- or 10-inch) baked pastry
  shell or graham cracker
  crumb crust*
6 egg yolks**
2 (14-ounce) cans Eagle® Brand
  Sweetened Condensed Milk
  (NOT evaporated milk)
1 (8-ounce) bottle ReaLime®
  Lime Juice from Concentrate
  Yellow or green food coloring,
  optional
  Whipped cream or whipped
  topping

Preheat oven to 350°. In large mixer
bowl, beat egg yolks with sweetened
condensed milk. Stir in ReaLime®
brand and food coloring if desired.
Pour into prepared pastry shell; bake
12 minutes. Cool. Chill. Top with
whipped cream. Garnish as desired.
Refrigerate leftovers.

KEY LIME MERINGUE PIE:
Omit whipped cream. Prepare filling
as above, reserving *4 egg whites;* do not
bake. In small mixer bowl, beat egg
whites with ¼ teaspoon cream of tartar
to soft peaks; gradually add ½ cup
sugar, beating until stiff but not dry.
Spread on top of pie, sealing carefully
to edge of pastry shell. Bake in
preheated 350° oven 15 minutes or
until lightly browned. Cool. Chill.

*If using frozen packaged pie shell
or 6-ounce packaged graham cracker
crumb pie crust, use 1 can Eagle®
Brand Sweetened Condensed Milk,
3 egg yolks and ½ cup ReaLime®
brand. Bake 8 minutes. Proceed as
above.

**Use only Grade A clean, uncracked
eggs.

COOL CREAMY PIES 73

Microwave Caramel Nut Cream Pie

REALEMON MERINGUE PIE

Makes one 9-inch pie

1 (9-inch) baked pastry shell
1⅔ cups sugar
6 tablespoons cornstarch
½ cup ReaLemon® Lemon Juice from Concentrate
4 eggs, separated*
1½ cups boiling water
2 tablespoons margarine or butter
¼ teaspoon cream of tartar

Preheat oven to 350°. In heavy saucepan, combine *1⅓ cups* sugar and cornstarch; add ReaLemon® brand. In small bowl, beat egg yolks; add to lemon mixture. Gradually add water, stirring constantly. Over medium heat, cook and stir until mixture boils and thickens, about 8 to 10 minutes. Remove from heat. Add margarine; stir until melted. Pour into prepared pastry shell. In small mixer bowl, beat egg whites with cream of tartar to soft peaks; gradually add remaining *⅓ cup* sugar, beating until stiff but not dry. Spread on top of pie, sealing carefully to edge of shell. Bake 12 to 15 minutes or until golden. Cool. Chill before serving. Garnish as desired. Refrigerate leftovers.

*Use only Grade A clean, uncracked eggs.

★ ★ ★ ★

MICROWAVE CARAMEL NUT CREAM PIE

Makes 1 pie

1 (14-ounce) can Eagle® Brand Sweetened Condensed Milk (NOT evaporated milk)
1 cup chopped nuts
2 tablespoons Borden® or Meadow Gold® Milk
½ teaspoon ground cinnamon
1 cup (½ pint) Borden® or Meadow Gold® Whipping Cream, whipped
1 (6-ounce) packaged graham cracker crumb pie crust

Pour sweetened condensed milk into 2-quart glass measure; cook on 50% power (medium) 4 minutes, stirring briskly every 2 minutes until smooth. Cook on 30% power (medium-low) 12 to 18 minutes or until very thick and caramel-colored, stirring briskly every 2 minutes until smooth. Stir nuts, milk and cinnamon into *warm* caramelized sweetened condensed milk; cool to room temperature. Fold in whipped cream. Pour into crust. Chill 3 hours or until set. Garnish as desired. Refrigerate leftovers.

ReaLemon Meringue Pie

★★★★
CANDY APPLE CHEESE PIE

Makes one 9-inch pie

1 (9-inch) baked pastry shell
1 (8-ounce) package cream cheese, softened
1 (14-ounce) can Eagle® Brand Sweetened Condensed Milk (NOT evaporated milk)
⅓ cup ReaLemon® Lemon Juice from Concentrate
1 teaspoon vanilla extract
1 (20-ounce) can sliced apples, *well drained* on paper towels
¼ cup red cinnamon candies
6 tablespoons water
2 teaspoons cornstarch

In large mixer bowl, beat cheese until fluffy. Gradually beat in sweetened condensed milk until smooth. Stir in ReaLemon® brand and vanilla. Pour into prepared pastry shell. Arrange apple slices over filling. In small saucepan, over *low* heat, dissolve cinnamon candies in ¼ *cup* water. Stir together remaining *2 tablespoons* water and cornstarch; add to cinnamon mixture. Cook and stir until mixture thickens and boils. Remove from heat; cool slightly. Drizzle over apples. Chill 3 hours or until set. Refrigerate leftovers.

★ ★ ★ ★

BANANA CREAM PIE

Makes one 9-inch pie

1 (9-inch) baked pastry shell
3 tablespoons cornstarch
¼ teaspoon salt
1⅔ cups water
1 (14-ounce) can Eagle® Brand
   Sweetened Condensed Milk
   (NOT evaporated milk)
3 egg yolks, beaten
2 tablespoons margarine or butter
1 teaspoon vanilla extract
3 medium bananas
   ReaLemon® Lemon Juice from
   Concentrate
1 cup (½ pint) Borden® or
   Meadow Gold® Whipping
   Cream, stiffly whipped

In heavy saucepan, dissolve cornstarch and salt in water; stir in sweetened condensed milk and egg yolks. Over medium heat, cook and stir until thickened and bubbly. Remove from heat; add margarine and vanilla. Cool slightly. Slice *2 bananas;* dip in ReaLemon® brand and drain. Arrange on bottom of prepared pastry shell. Pour filling over bananas; cover. Chill 4 hours or until set. Spread top with whipped cream. Slice remaining banana; dip in ReaLemon® brand, drain and garnish top of pie. Refrigerate leftovers.

MICROWAVE: In 2-quart glass measure, combine cornstarch, salt, water, sweetened condensed milk and egg yolks as above. Cook on 100% power (high) 5 to 6 minutes, stirring after 3 minutes then after each minute until thickened. Proceed as above.

Strawberry Cheese Pie

LEMON KIWIFRUIT PIE

Makes one 9-inch pie

1 (9-inch) baked pastry shell
1 (14-ounce) can Eagle® Brand
    Sweetened Condensed Milk
    (NOT evaporated milk)
1 (6-ounce) can frozen lemonade
    or limeade concentrate,
    thawed
    Yellow food coloring, optional
1 (8-ounce) container frozen non-
    dairy whipped topping,
    thawed (3½ cups)
2 kiwifruit, peeled and sliced

In large bowl, combine sweetened condensed milk, lemonade concentrate and food coloring if desired; mix well. Fold in whipped topping. Pour into prepared pastry shell. Chill 4 hours or until set. Garnish with kiwifruit. Refrigerate leftovers.

★★★★

STRAWBERRY CHEESE PIE

Makes one 9-inch pie

1 (9-inch) baked pastry shell or
    graham cracker crumb crust
1 (8-ounce) package cream cheese,
    softened
1 (14-ounce) can Eagle® Brand
    Sweetened Condensed Milk
    (NOT evaporated milk)
⅓ cup ReaLemon® Lemon Juice
    from Concentrate
1 teaspoon vanilla extract
1 quart fresh strawberries,
    cleaned and hulled
    (about 1½ pounds)
1 (16-ounce) package prepared
    strawberry glaze, chilled

In large mixer bowl, beat cheese until fluffy. Gradually beat in sweetened condensed milk until smooth. Stir in ReaLemon® brand and vanilla. Pour into prepared pastry shell. Chill 3 hours or until set. Top with strawberries and desired amount of glaze. Refrigerate leftovers.

Lemon Kiwifruit Pie

━━━━━ ★★★★ ━━━━━

CHERRY ALMOND MOUSSE PIE

Makes one 9-inch pie

1 (9-inch) baked pastry shell
1 (1-ounce) square unsweetened
    chocolate
1 (14-ounce) can Eagle® Brand
    Sweetened Condensed Milk
    (NOT evaporated milk)
1 teaspoon almond extract
1 (8-ounce) package cream cheese,
    softened
1 cup cold water
1 (4-serving size) package *instant*
    vanilla flavor pudding mix
1 cup (½ pint) Borden® or
    Meadow Gold® Whipping
    Cream, whipped
1 (10-ounce) jar red maraschino
    cherries, well drained,
    reserving 5 or 6 for garnish,
    chop remainder
½ cup chopped toasted almonds
    Additional almonds and
    chocolate curls

In heavy saucepan, over low heat, melt chocolate with *½ cup* sweetened condensed milk until thickened; stir in *¼ teaspoon* almond extract. Spread on bottom of prepared pastry shell. In large mixer bowl, beat cheese until fluffy. Gradually beat in remaining sweetened condensed milk then water, pudding mix and remaining *¾ teaspoon* almond extract. Fold in whipped cream, chopped cherries and almonds. Pour into prepared pastry shell. Chill 4 hours or until set. Garnish with reserved cherries, additional almonds and chocolate curls. Refrigerate leftovers.

★★★★
FLUFFY LEMON CHEESE PIE

Makes one 9-inch pie

1 (9-inch) baked pastry shell
2 eggs, separated*
1¼ cups sugar
⅓ cup cornstarch
1 cup water
⅓ cup ReaLemon® Lemon Juice
   from Concentrate
1 (3-ounce) package cream cheese,
   softened
Raspberry Sauce

In small bowl, beat egg yolks. In medium saucepan, combine *1 cup* sugar and cornstarch; add water, ReaLemon® brand and egg yolks. Over low heat, cook and stir until thickened. Remove from heat. Add cheese; mix well. Cool to room temperature. In small mixer bowl, beat egg whites to soft peaks; gradually add remaining *¼ cup* sugar, beating until stiff but not dry. Fold into lemon mixture; pour into prepared pastry shell. Chill 4 hours or until set. Serve with Raspberry Sauce. Refrigerate leftovers.

RASPBERRY SAUCE: In small saucepan, combine syrup drained from 1 (10-ounce) package thawed frozen red raspberries and 2 teaspoons cornstarch. Cook and stir until thickened and clear. Stir in raspberries. Chill. (Makes about 1 cup)

MICROWAVE: In 2-cup glass measure, combine reserved raspberry syrup and 2 teaspoons cornstarch; mix well. Cook on 100% power (high) 2 to 4 minutes or until thickened, stirring after each minute. Stir in raspberries. Chill. (Makes about 1 cup)

*Use only Grade A clean, uncracked eggs.

====★★★★====

MICROWAVE ORANGE CREAM PIE

Makes one 9-inch pie

1½ cups gingersnap cookie crumbs
   (about 28 cookies)
6 tablespoons margarine or
   butter, melted
1 (14-ounce) can Eagle® Brand
   Sweetened Condensed Milk
   (NOT evaporated milk)
¼ cup frozen orange juice
   concentrate, thawed
2 egg yolks
2 teaspoons grated orange rind
1 (8-ounce) container Borden® or
   Meadow Gold® Sour Cream,
   at room temperature
Whipped topping

Combine crumbs and margarine; press firmly on bottom and up side to rim of microwavable pie plate. Cook on 100% power (high) 2 minutes, rotating plate after 1 minute. Cool. Meanwhile, in 2-quart glass measure, mix sweetened condensed milk, juice concentrate, egg yolks and rind; cook on 100% power (high) 3 to 4 minutes, stirring after 2 minutes. Cool 10 minutes; stir in sour cream. Pour into prepared crust. Chill 3 hours or until set. Spread with whipped topping; garnish as desired. Refrigerate leftovers.

★ ★ ★ ★

STRAWBERRY DAIQUIRI PIE

Makes one 9-inch pie

1 (9-inch) graham cracker crumb crust or baked pastry shell
1 (8-ounce) package cream cheese, softened
1 (14-ounce) can Eagle® Brand Sweetened Condensed Milk (NOT evaporated milk)
⅔ cup frozen strawberry daiquiri mix, thawed
2 tablespoons light rum
Red food coloring, optional
1 cup (½ pint) Borden® or Meadow Gold® Whipping Cream, whipped

In large mixer bowl, beat cheese until fluffy. Gradually beat in sweetened condensed milk until smooth. Stir in daiquiri mix, rum and food coloring if desired. Fold in whipped cream. Pour into prepared crust. Chill or freeze 4 hours or until firm. Garnish as desired. Refrigerate or freeze leftovers.

LIME DAIQUIRI PIE: Omit strawberry daiquiri mix and red food coloring. Add ¼ cup ReaLime® Lime Juice from Concentrate and a few drops green food coloring if desired. Proceed as above.

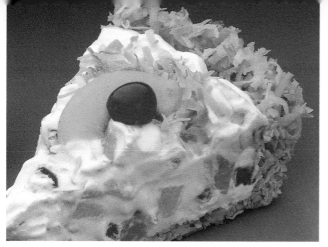

Ambrosia Pie

★★★★
CHOCOLATE TRUFFLE PIE

Makes one 9- or 10-inch pie

1 (9- or 10-inch) chocolate crumb crust
1 envelope unflavored gelatine
½ cup water
3 (1-ounce) squares unsweetened or semi-sweet chocolate, melted and cooled
1 (14-ounce) can Eagle® Brand Sweetened Condensed Milk (NOT evaporated milk)
1 teaspoon vanilla extract
2 cups (1 pint) Borden® or Meadow Gold® Whipping Cream, whipped

In small saucepan, sprinkle gelatine over water; let stand 1 minute. Over low heat, stir until gelatine dissolves. Cool. In large mixer bowl, beat chocolate with sweetened condensed milk until smooth. Stir in gelatine mixture and vanilla. Fold in whipped cream. Pour into prepared crust. Chill 3 hours or until set. Garnish as desired. Refrigerate leftovers.

★★★★
AMBROSIA PIE

Makes one 9-inch pie

1 (7-ounce) package flaked coconut (2⅔ cups), toasted
⅓ cup margarine or butter, melted
1 (14-ounce) can Eagle® Brand Sweetened Condensed Milk (NOT evaporated milk)
⅓ cup ReaLemon® Lemon Juice from Concentrate
1 (17-ounce) can fruit cocktail, *well drained*
½ cup slivered almonds, toasted and chopped
¼ cup chopped maraschino cherries, well drained
1 (4-ounce) container frozen non-dairy whipped topping, thawed (1¾ cups)
Additional fruit, optional

Combine coconut and margarine. Reserving 2 tablespoons coconut mixture, press remainder firmly on bottom and up side to rim of 9-inch pie plate. Chill. In large bowl, combine sweetened condensed milk, ReaLemon® brand, fruit cocktail, almonds and cherries; mix well. Fold in whipped topping. Pour into prepared crust. Chill 4 hours or until set. Garnish with reserved coconut and additional fruit if desired. Refrigerate leftovers.

Chocolate Truffle Pie

PEPPERMINT PARFAIT PIE

Makes one 9-inch pie

1 (9-inch) baked pastry shell
1 (1-ounce) square unsweetened
   chocolate
1 (14-ounce) can Eagle® Brand
   Sweetened Condensed Milk
   (NOT evaporated milk)
½ teaspoon vanilla extract
1 (8-ounce) package cream cheese,
   softened
3 tablespoons white creme
   de menthe
   Red food coloring, optional
1 (8-ounce) container frozen non-
   dairy whipped topping,
   thawed (3½ cups)

In small saucepan, melt chocolate with ½ *cup* sweetened condensed milk; stir in vanilla. Spread on bottom of prepared pastry shell. In large mixer bowl, beat cheese until fluffy. Gradually beat in remaining sweetened condensed milk. Stir in creme de menthe and food coloring if desired. Fold in whipped topping. Pour into prepared pastry shell. Chill 4 hours or until set. Garnish as desired. Refrigerate leftovers.

★★★★

NESSELRODE CREAM PIE

Makes one 9-inch pie

Chocolate Coconut Crust
1 envelope unflavored gelatine
¼ cup water
1 (14-ounce) can Eagle® Brand Sweetened Condensed Milk (NOT evaporated milk)
¼ cup Borden® or Meadow Gold® Sour Cream
2 tablespoons light rum
½ cup chopped mixed candied fruit
½ cup chopped nuts
¼ cup raisins
2 teaspoons grated orange rind
1 cup (½ pint) Borden® or Meadow Gold® Whipping Cream, whipped

Prepare Chocolate Coconut Crust. In small saucepan, sprinkle gelatine over water; let stand 1 minute. Over low heat, stir until gelatine dissolves. In large bowl, combine sweetened condensed milk, sour cream, gelatine mixture and rum. Chill until mixture mounds slightly when dropped from spoon, about 15 minutes. Fold in fruit, nuts, raisins, rind then whipped cream. Pour into prepared crust. Chill 4 hours or until set. Garnish as desired. Refrigerate leftovers.

CHOCOLATE COCONUT CRUST: In large saucepan, over low heat, melt 2 tablespoons margarine or butter with 1 (1-ounce) square semisweet chocolate. Add 1 (7-ounce) package flaked coconut (2⅔ cups); mix well. Press firmly on bottom and up side to rim of buttered 9-inch pie plate. Chill.

==★★★★==

BANANA SPLIT
DESSERT PIZZA

Makes one 12-inch pizza

1 (14-ounce) can Eagle® Brand
   Sweetened Condensed Milk
   (NOT evaporated milk)
½ cup Borden® or Meadow Gold®
   Sour Cream
6 tablespoons ReaLemon® Lemon
   Juice from Concentrate
1 teaspoon vanilla extract
½ cup plus 1 tablespoon margarine
   or butter, softened
¼ cup firmly packed brown sugar
1 cup unsifted flour
¼ cup quick-cooking oats
¼ cup finely chopped nuts
3 medium bananas
1 (8-ounce) can sliced pineapple,
   drained and cut in half
   Maraschino cherries and nuts
1 (1-ounce) square semi-sweet
   chocolate

Preheat oven to 375°. In medium bowl, combine sweetened condensed milk, sour cream, ¼ *cup* ReaLemon® brand and vanilla; mix well. Chill. In large mixer bowl, beat ½ *cup* margarine and sugar until fluffy; add flour, oats and nuts. Mix well. On lightly greased pizza pan or baking sheet, press dough into 12-inch circle, forming rim around edge. Prick with fork. Bake 10 to 12 minutes or until golden brown. Cool. Slice bananas; arrange *2 bananas* on cooled crust. Spoon filling evenly over bananas. Dip remaining banana slices in remaining *2 tablespoons* ReaLemon® brand; drain and arrange on top along with pineapple, cherries and additional nuts. In small saucepan, over low heat, melt chocolate with remaining *1 tablespoon* margarine; drizzle over pie. Chill thoroughly. Refrigerate leftovers.

TIP: Crust and filling can be made in advance. Store crust at room temperature; refrigerate filling.

Raspberry-Topped Lemon Pie

★★★★

LIME CREAM PIE

Makes 1 pie

1 (14-ounce) can Eagle® Brand
    Sweetened Condensed Milk
    (NOT evaporated milk)
½ cup ReaLime® Lime Juice from
    Concentrate
    Green food coloring, optional
1 cup (½ pint) Borden® or
    Meadow Gold® Whipping
    Cream, whipped
1 (6-ounce) packaged graham
    cracker crumb pie crust

In medium bowl, stir together
sweetened condensed milk, ReaLime®
brand and food coloring if desired.
Fold in whipped cream. Pour into
crust. Chill 3 hours or until set.
Garnish as desired. Refrigerate
leftovers.

LEMON CREAM PIE: Substitute
½ cup ReaLemon® Lemon Juice from
Concentrate for ReaLime® brand.

★★★★

RASPBERRY-TOPPED LEMON PIE

Makes 1 pie

1 (10-ounce) package frozen red
    raspberries in syrup, thawed
1 tablespoon cornstarch
3 egg yolks*
1 (14-ounce) can Eagle® Brand
    Sweetened Condensed Milk
    (NOT evaporated milk)
½ cup ReaLemon® Lemon Juice
    from Concentrate
    Yellow food coloring, optional
1 (6-ounce) packaged graham
    cracker crumb pie crust
    Whipped topping

Preheat oven to 350°. In small
saucepan, combine raspberries
and cornstarch; cook and stir until
thickened and clear. In medium bowl,
beat egg yolks; stir in sweetened
condensed milk, ReaLemon® brand
and food coloring if desired. Pour
into crust; bake 8 minutes. Spoon
raspberry mixture evenly over top.
Chill 4 hours or until set. Spread with
whipped topping. Garnish as desired.
Refrigerate leftovers.

*Use only Grade A clean, uncracked
eggs.

Lime Cream Pie

BROWNIE FRUIT PIZZA

Makes one 12-inch pizza

- 1 (12.9- or 15-ounce) package fudge brownie mix
- 1 (8-ounce) package cream cheese, softened
- 1 (14-ounce) can Eagle® Brand Sweetened Condensed Milk (NOT evaporated milk)
- ½ cup frozen pineapple *or* orange juice concentrate, thawed
- 1 teaspoon vanilla extract
  Assorted fresh or canned fruit (strawberries, bananas, kiwifruit, orange, pineapple, etc.)

Preheat oven to 350°. Prepare brownie mix as package directs. On greased pizza pan or baking sheet, spread batter into 12-inch circle. Bake 15 to 20 minutes. Meanwhile, in small mixer bowl, beat cheese until fluffy. Gradually beat in sweetened condensed milk until smooth. Stir in juice concentrate and vanilla. Chill thoroughly. Just before serving, spoon filling over cooled brownie crust. Arrange fruit on top. Refrigerate leftovers.

Quick Butterscotch Cheese Pie

QUICK BUTTERSCOTCH CHEESE PIE

Makes one 9-inch pie

- 1 (9-inch) baked pastry shell or graham cracker crumb crust
- 1 (8-ounce) package cream cheese, softened
- 1 (14-ounce) can Eagle® Brand Sweetened Condensed Milk (NOT evaporated milk)
- ¾ cup cold water
- 1 (4-serving size) package *instant* butterscotch flavor pudding mix
- 1 cup (½ pint) Borden® or Meadow Gold® Whipping Cream, whipped

In large mixer bowl, beat cheese until fluffy; gradually beat in sweetened condensed milk until smooth. On low speed, beat in water and pudding mix until smooth. Fold in whipped cream. Pour into prepared pastry shell. Chill 2 hours or until set. Garnish as desired. Refrigerate leftovers.

CHOCOLATE CHEESE PIE: Substitute *instant* chocolate flavor pudding mix for butterscotch. Add ¼ cup unsweetened cocoa with pudding mix. Proceed as above.

COCONUT CHEESE PIE: Substitute *instant* coconut cream flavor pudding mix for butterscotch. Fold in ½ cup flaked coconut with whipped cream. Proceed as above.

VANILLA NUT CHEESE PIE: Substitute *instant* vanilla flavor pudding mix for butterscotch. Fold in ¾ cup chopped toasted nuts with whipped cream. Proceed as above.

★ ★ ★ ★

CREAMY LEMON PIE

Makes one 8- or 9-inch pie

1 (8- or 9-inch) baked pastry shell
  or graham cracker crumb
  crust
3 egg yolks*
1 (14-ounce) can Eagle® Brand
  Sweetened Condensed Milk
  (NOT evaporated milk)
½ cup ReaLemon® Lemon Juice
  from Concentrate
  Yellow food coloring, optional
  Whipped topping or whipped
  cream

Preheat oven to 350°. In medium bowl, beat egg yolks; stir in sweetened condensed milk, ReaLemon® brand and food coloring if desired. Pour into prepared pastry shell; bake 8 minutes. Cool. Chill. Spread with whipped topping. Garnish as desired. Refrigerate leftovers.

CREAMY LEMON MERINGUE PIE: Omit whipped topping. Prepare filling as above, reserving egg whites; do not bake. In small mixer bowl, beat egg whites with ¼ teaspoon cream of tartar to soft peaks; gradually add ⅓ cup sugar, beating until stiff but not dry. Spread on top of pie, sealing carefully to edge of pastry shell. Bake in preheated 350° oven 12 to 15 minutes or until golden brown. Cool. Chill.

*Use only Grade A clean, uncracked eggs.

PIE MAKING HINTS

★★★★

PASTRY CRUST

Makes one 8- or 9-inch crust

1 cup unsifted flour
½ teaspoon salt
⅓ cup shortening
3 to 4 tablespoons cold water

In medium bowl, combine flour and salt; cut in shortening until crumbly. Sprinkle with water, 1 tablespoon at a time, mixing until dough is just moist enough to hold together. Form into ball. On floured surface, press dough down into a flat circle with smooth edges. Roll out into a circle ⅛ inch thick and about 1½ inches larger than inverted pie plate. Ease dough into pie plate. Trim ½ inch beyond pie plate edge. Fold under; flute edge as desired.

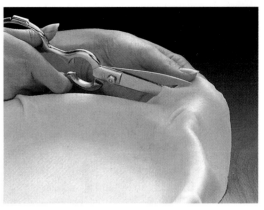

Use kitchen shears or sharp knife to trim dough ½ inch beyond pie plate edge. Fold under extra dough to form rim.

★★★★

TO BAKE WITHOUT FILLING

Preheat oven to 450°. Prick bottom and side of pastry shell with fork. Line pastry with aluminum foil; fill with dry beans. Bake 5 minutes; remove beans and foil. Bake 5 to 7 minutes longer or until golden.

Flute edge as desired.

★★★★

TO BAKE WITH FILLING

Preheat oven as directed in recipe. Do not prick pastry shell. Fill and bake as directed.

To keep an unfilled pastry crust from puffing or shrinking during baking, line with aluminum foil and fill with dry beans.

★ ★ ★ ★
LEMON PASTRY

Makes one 9-inch pastry crust

1 cup unsifted flour
½ teaspoon salt
⅓ cup shortening
1 egg, beaten
1 tablespoon ReaLemon® Lemon
  Juice from Concentrate

Preheat oven to 400°. In medium bowl, combine flour and salt; cut in shortening until crumbly. In small bowl, beat egg and ReaLemon® brand. Sprinkle over flour mixture; stir until dough forms a ball. On floured surface, roll out to a circle ⅛ inch thick and about 1½ inches larger than inverted pie plate. Ease dough into pie plate. Trim ½ inch beyond pie plate edge. Fold under; flute edge as desired. Prick with fork. Bake 12 to 15 minutes or until golden.

★ ★ ★ ★
CRUMB CRUST

Makes one 8- or 9-inch crust

1½ cups graham cracker or
    chocolate wafer crumbs
¼ cup sugar
6 tablespoons margarine or
    butter, melted

Combine ingredients; mix well. Press firmly on bottom and up side to rim of 8- or 9-inch pie plate. Chill thoroughly or bake in preheated 375° oven 6 to 8 minutes or until edges are brown. Cool before filling.

★ ★ ★ ★
APPLES FOR PIE

To give ordinary eating apples the tartness of "pie apples," sprinkle 1 tablespoon ReaLemon® Lemon Juice from Concentrate over sliced apples.

★ ★ ★ ★
PASTRY EGG WASH

For a more golden crust on a 2-crust pie, beat 1 egg yolk with 2 tablespoons water; brush evenly over pastry before baking.

★ ★ ★ ★
TOASTING COCONUT AND NUTS

CONVENTIONAL OVEN: Spread coconut or nuts in shallow pan. Toast in preheated 350° oven 7 to 15 minutes or until golden, stirring frequently.

MICROWAVE OVEN:

Coconut: Spread ½ cup coconut in glass pie plate. Cook on 70% power (medium-high) 5 to 10 minutes or until lightly browned, stirring after each minute.

Nuts: Spread 1 cup nuts in glass pie plate. Cook on 100% power (high) 5 to 8 minutes or until lightly browned, stirring after each minute.

NOTE: In microwave oven, nuts heat quickly and brown evenly. Remove from oven as soon as they begin to brown (browning will continue as they stand). Pie plate and nuts will be very hot after toasting; handle carefully.

Beat whipping cream only until *stiff* peaks form.

━━━━━━★★★★━━━━━━

WHIPPING CREAM

Chill beaters and bowl thoroughly.

Beat chilled whipping cream on high speed (overbeating or beating on low speed can cause cream to separate into fat and liquid).

Beat only until stiff. Whipping cream doubles in volume.

━━━━━━★★★★━━━━━━

SWEETENED WHIPPED CREAM

Makes about 2 cups

1 cup (½ pint) Borden® or
    Meadow Gold® Whipping
    Cream
1 to 2 tablespoons sugar
½ to 1 teaspoon vanilla extract

In small mixer bowl, beat cream to soft peaks; gradually add sugar and vanilla, beating until stiff. Refrigerate leftovers.

WHIPPED CREAM FLAVOR VARIATIONS:

Chocolate: Increase sugar to 4 tablespoons. Add 1 to 2 tablespoons unsweetened cocoa to unwhipped cream; proceed as above.

Lemon: Omit vanilla; use 2 tablespoons sugar. Add 1 tablespoon ReaLemon® Lemon Juice from Concentrate to unwhipped cream; proceed as above.

Coffee: Add ½ to 1 teaspoon instant coffee to unwhipped cream; proceed as above.

Cinnamon: Add ¼ to ½ teaspoon ground cinnamon to unwhipped cream; proceed as above.

Peppermint: Omit vanilla. Add ½ teaspoon peppermint extract along with sugar; proceed as above.

━━━━━━★★★★━━━━━━

MAPLE WHIPPED CREAM

Makes about 2 cups

1 cup (½ pint) Borden® or
    Meadow Gold® Whipping
    Cream
¼ cup Cary's®, Vermont Maple
    Orchards or MacDonald's
    Pure Maple Syrup

In small mixer bowl, beat cream and syrup until stiff. Refrigerate leftovers.

★★★★
FOR SUCCESSFUL MERINGUE

Weather affects meringues. When the humidity is high, the sugar in the meringue absorbs moisture from the air, making the meringue gooey and limp. Meringues should be made on sunny, dry days.

Carefully separate egg whites from the yolks (they separate best when cold).

Mixing bowls and beaters should be completely grease-free.

Egg whites should come to room temperature before beating. This increases the volume.

Sugar should be added *gradually.* Continue beating until sugar is completely dissolved.

Cool meringue slowly, away from drafts to prevent shrinking and weeping.

★★★★
MERINGUE

For 8- or 9-inch pie

3 egg whites
¼ teaspoon cream of tartar
6 tablespoons sugar

Preheat oven to 350°. In small mixer bowl, beat egg whites with cream of tartar to soft peaks; gradually add sugar, beating until stiff but not dry. Spread meringue on top of pie, sealing carefully to edge of pastry shell. Bake 12 to 15 minutes or until lightly browned. Cool. Chill.

1. Beat egg whites and cream of tartar to *soft peaks* before adding sugar.

2. *Gradually* add sugar, beating until *stiff* but not dry. Mixture should be glossy.

3. Spread meringue, sealing carefully to edge of pastry shell.

4. Brown meringue as directed. Cool *slowly.*

★ INDEX ★